THE ALL-UNION DAY
OF THE SHOCK WORKER

Also by Edwin Torres

I Hear Things People Haven't Really Said (1991)
Lung Poetry (1994)
SandHomméNomadNo (1997)
Fractured Humorous (1999)
Onomalingua: noise songs and poetry (2000)

CD
Holy Kid (1998)

THE
ALL-UNION DAY
OF THE
SHOCK WORKER

EDWIN TORRES

ROOF BOOKS
NEW YORK

Book design: Edwin Torres
Shock Worker drawing: Elizabeth Castagna

ACKNOWLEDGEMENTS: *Unfinished Beginnings* was written as part of a collaborative project with the artist Suzanne McClelland. The poems emerged from dialogues and painting sessions using unfinished beginnings as a theme. *What What What Now* was written based on Steve Cannon's play, *What Now Now What*. Each poem is a scene and was conducted by Butch Morris along with 4 other poet's interpretation of the play, while the play itself was performed—the poems in effect were a sound score to the play. *Canyon Suite* was written in the same manner. *I.E.Zagmm* is a re-translation of my poem *I.E.Seducer* published in the anthology *Aloud*. Some of these pieces first appeared in the following publications: *Big City Lit, Washington Post Review, Longshot Magazine, Rebel Road* and *Kenning*.

Thanks to James Sherry for his guidance; Steve Cannon, Suzanne McLelland, Bill Goldston & Universal Limited Art Editions, and Butch Morris who were influential to the writing in this book; and to the New York Foundation for the Arts, The Poetry Fund and the Foundation for Contemporary Performance Art for their support.

A special thank you to my family and friends who continue to give me unparallelled support and to Elizabeth for her never-ending wonder.

 This book was made possible, in part, by a grant from the New York State Council on the Arts.

ROOF BOOKS
are published by
Segue Foundation
303 East 8th Street
New York, NY 10009
www.segue.org

This Is The Glass Unlit
By A Dolphin To My Side / 7

UNFINISHED BEGINNINGS

Separatist Invasion / 36

WHAT WHAT WHAT NOW

A Building Of Voice / 57
Bone Boy / 58

CANYON SUITE: A PARALLEL TEXT IN FIVE ACTS

A Man Of Two / 76
The Energy Of Matter Accelerated / 77

I.E. ZAGMM

Intrinite Line / 88

A NUYO-FUTURISTS' MANIFESTINY

THIS IS THE GLASS UNLIT BY A DOLPHIN TO MY SIDE

       may I matter—and dislike
       the everyway—of am
       may I make a matter—into
       everyway I am—may I
       like this—and want
       to figure out—this roll
       I am fired by

Jumping from the fire
into the fire—voice of glass that
breaks this eardrumhole

Let this hole—let it be
reflected
off this pierced phantasm

Mantra of a man
in glassed maligna

Childless wonder
at home
in arms of world

       size matters—when you're different
       sez the skinny boy—biting onna moon pie
       carressing his mother's cheek—her face in his palm

             glass that fires   *into a dolphin's blowhole*
    glass that wants to shatter   *in a dolphin*
          glass that keeps   *dolphin afloat*
           glass is my voice   *at work against my hold*

This is the mantra
of a man unglassed—I was
in wonder of my skinny arms

All along
it was my voice
that was shattered

UNFINISHED

•

BEGINNINGS

(QUa)

eye for eyetooth

in a box of us

sunlight

is our stage   *start to finish*

            in the losing shadows

            we spray what

we COLOR *we*

what spray we

shadows

in the losing finish

to start stage   *ours is*

            sunlight in a box ● **UNBEGINNING**

            of us tootheye

            foreye

"IS A FIND"

i finish to be finish once again

as a man i have yet to throw away girl

as i begin i have yet to know a way out

as i have yet to lose boy as a woman i saw girl be

as i boy her to me to once again

to own what i lose

"THE EXPECT OF SPACE"

What could trigger more involve?
Might that involve
more involve, mighty...to make again
the expect of space?

In slays, the fall is mighty.
Though my edge is aligned to correct I expect
a remember of voices to cross my way.
A bath of involve space.

The gash of sound.
Shape rather than Shadow.
The invite space.
The finite present.
A drop of tar, a plod...may I leave it
only as to gain begin again?

Drawn to quarterly fame
I am Same and As in one.
Other and Edge in you.
String to whistle scarred.
Strong to finish, I need to leave it...
yet—I nor to what I need again.

I am along and gone.
The scratch on air.
I am the again that falls.

"LAST"

Who-be-that looks at who-you-be
skinnier than me, they would win.
Would always have the break of it
chance taken is rewarded with chance given.

Since was once awhile ago,
scared of it, grown and wanting.
We see what wants *Since*
and what wants *Was,*
sees me, hugs me, in a not-let-go.

      She is filled out to cloud cheeks
      that hold back at times
      what she wants for her children.
      A sound I didn't know I had, calls me
      from long ago when I heard her snore
      and thought something wrong, so
      I covered her mouth startling her awake.
      What's wrong? she asked.
      I just looked at her embarrassed
      and went back to sleep.

She, looking at me in the morning.
A look I didn't know I needed.

"A ONCE AWHILE SINCE"

Yolk'um grab a grist!
The skin is pulled off in fistfoot curlies lookit BAM!
The sky is a skinscab in chunks.
You think you don't need anymore and BAM!

> *why aren't you with me?*
> *why aren't you with me?*
> *why aren't you with me?*
> > *do I care for the fall of yo(u)?*
> > *a U braced under collapse of dead sky?*
> > *gotten in the way of good fresh sky?...BAM!*

Repetition is an affirming thing.
The *itit* of it reclaims by a slight shift
a once awhile since.

TO *GO* WHEN YOU'RE FIRST
LAST TO *LASTING* BUT MOSTLY *FIRSTLINGS*
WHY MUST *WHY* ITSELF THROUGH STINK
THE *FILL* OF YOU—SO *FULL* OF YOU
NOWHERE IS THERE ONLY *ONE*

{ *One sits   Two calls   Three lies   Says One left*
Two goes   One sits   Three...pretends not to see
One believes in Me, so...Why must believe in One   No? } ...*BAM!*

O I am the darkly I've heard about.
Retch! Connive myself
sing a hairnote from the bonnet, Asphyxiate of D.

I can't hear the birds
but that's only 'cause my head is low.
                   It's a slow crawl through me
a smell I didn't know I wanted.
                   It's very, an explosion kind, just...a linger of such sounds
                   I didn't know I needed.

A SKINDRIP OF SKY—THE CRUMBLE HOLDS HER CROUCH
TWO FIFTY CENTS—SLAYERED TO *S* FOREVER
FOR STRUCTURAL REASONS
THE *F* AS A *P*—THE DITTO PROJECTION

Now that I feel all over, a well-worn feel
            it is my dollar Coke that I leave willy-nilly Balzac
                                                (...bam!)

Below the surface, capillaries form
rabbits and horsies in the wind. Varicose sunsets
slightly wounded, signify
previously perilous encounters.

            O I ease the breath offa generation.
            FE's another *E*-male, the remaining light pulled.
            Good covered by dark, obscured by dead clouds
            trying to grow by the bump of dead skin.

            O this hollow walk, no? To be seen
            for what I do, do I need instead
            what I am?

(APp)

In the space here before me
Immersed in no light - assa sars &
A gaggle of R's march

NEW YORK SKYLINE
JUMBLING INDIFFERENT TOXIC MUMBLES
TAXIC YELLOW BUCKETS
GASSING TRANSPORT CITY OF CLAY
SANDBLASTED SOLIO

My home is the open shadow, I visit
Every chance I get

I splatch my furnished Re's
(about to) members a silent rain
A hmmmpf & I'm off

On a squared napkinate philo-so-so-fianical
Is my coloration - macnellcoltration,
A chance...(*COME HERE, AND)*
To bucket the floor - with the color
Of stars

● FALLEN APPLE MISTAKEN FOR A WISH

16

"THE FIRST OF IT"

I hear speech mine and how I hear in my mother
        (now ya know)
Maybe the generation of breath through repetition
Is where another pulse comes from
        (heh heh)
The first of baby firstlings: e^d b^eg unfinish_{ing}s
        (tha sky's acummin')

      i was born
      i was born
      born into the night

      i was born
      i was born
      born into this light

      i was born
      i was born
      a scot rat bastard

      the man o' the pidgy's
      in the whyte o' his wings
      an' i'm a chicky me one day...heh heh
      fly baby buh buh

      i was love
      i was love
      i was love

"UNION"

Unfit Intessimal Sublimat-Wat!
Tee's Inginning Sur-Be's!
Fornint Tess! F after IN
on a platform showcasing the The.

"A DIDN'T SAME"

between word and breath I bit...YUCK!

The convince of hearing the same words
over
is that you hear the same spaces between the same
over
the same convince of words as same
as
the spaces you just heard that you hear

Another breath between the didn'ts
a breath I didn't know
I had to take another breath I didn't
know I needed
one I didn't know was available

Another word I didn't know
I needed another sound
I didn't existed another want
I didn't word
A don't know I didn't need
another skin I don't

(ODo)

repetition is a very
comforting suffer
-ing people laugh more
it takes the place of
time replaces medicine
medical discovery is
humor incurable my socks
are insuffffffffferable yet veeeeery
comforting I hav mannnnny
socks repetititious socks
are my comforting hole
I like repeating things
in oddd places

● THE COMFORT OF ODD PLACES ▬▬▬▬▬▬▬▬

(FRe)

I am, maybe an oldist
a roller coaster, but
somehow the thing of
dropping...adventurist
isn't it!

Straight down curve
g-force poodlebrawn
I'm only an oldist in the
freefall, mind traveling
in the bodysmack!

● **G-FORCE CULEMBRA**

(NOo)

Our stage is sunlight
we color our spray
with using—*start for finish*
who's around us—*eye for eyetooth*
in a box of us, the room
becomes story
   ...oaf! who(m) uses
      losing shadows anymyre...retch!

In the sinced sense
the would-be Shale Conqueror
is the go-out June-er,
the Summer Camp Do-er
is the would-be Princess, and some rains
would call her home, once upon a home
   oaf...& I, am I to
      continue this sculpture...yoaf
        a castle-story!
   & it's all & only
      how I know...moaf!

Our love is designed
to divide up time into many parts

Where *last* might be
flesh-colored windows parting
to see curtainy
mehole for eyehole... **UPSIDE**
        SMILEFACE
         ACIDALL
         OUTPIE
          DOWN

● **ON THE LAYERS OF A SECRET**
(*a fairee tail for nary none a 'ya*)

On a template for a wish...

       Who breaks ebony for coal (?)

       Who's mattressa licks grippera (?)

       Who's romp is a moment *in-viscera* (?)

...that is—to be the moment

that gains momentum

by including its mistake—(*sss*)

       sunburst eyelashes—shared for the given life

& oh, let's explore—& what one takes

is another's stomp

       With stillness—our body is a way to write

       speaking silent vibration

       This is to seem—as if writing

       were the *spell* of air

       Buckets of since-layerings washed in secret

       2 letters of magical sound

       Sculpted Sonarias

       Ravenous Houdinis

Some might say...

our story overlooks the majestic rhyme

that lies in rivers of effervescent conques-*soaring*

Perhaps—

Mirror Goop Grab, if a wet faith

is Scubbard Droop *THEN* it is proud, as we

take a bow

pssst...another effortless favorite of ours— *allowed flaws and* *nursery dittos* *clayish and meltish—*
while answering the roll *off the tongue*

In the hours short of a big 'a-rilla...
    Who breaks the back
    reading e-nuts, gutter sop, and fancy (?)
    A neckless Prince (?) *whince...*
    A naked Princess (?)
    Hours shared exploring mistakes (?)
    And how each one takes the other's stomp (?)

In the sinced sense—we all had *enjoy*
flattered by beauty-sound
Exotic suntown twines about me—would be crimson
to the west but our night is sealed,
quirled to a brighter day

When closed in, we storm the kiss of the first muscle
The pattern followed—will leave
with morning's invention—dewdrop's intention
In the cliffs of our story
our *Once* overlooks an age of long twilight

Our speech is designed in since time
in the skim of a separating sense—we spray

pssst...will somebody tell the peanut butter occulist

dishing dollops by ivory palms...won't somebody

give the very olive chim-cherry arms...come now can't somebody anybody won't anyone have

something to say...to the, oh...there's a maybe where we

go...oh, where is there

a...yessy...maybe...oh!

(G'Do)

JULIO.B.O.MIET

region of squirt
hullo, I am Robo-Jerk
fang of Comaria
byte bot
hulloh, I am Eye-Joke
nose of you, I dot
window to my rot
holluh, I be I-Bot
washing sunlight witta
fecal toke, bubba-pleen
cartooning outta chomp
I splurt g'dow
hullo, I am Ro-Me-Ot

(oRSe)

HORSEBOY TILLS HIS HEART IN CATTLE LAND

Gladys-mad as Shine
Lad of Love an Ox
of Monarchy my
Narchy Ray offa course
offsteer 'causa Course away
To stain the Eyelash Boon
in 7 Horns in built in Suuuns
Her 7 tunes inside'er graze
or ABZ to Stay where
Hilltop makes the Box
to Frame idolatry Or maybe
Course the Peasant pulling Hard
on token Gladys

WERE MI FIERCE USSLE

a
Grimmace
        from a
Gydrannce

I used to like to repeat things alot
Then I got bored
I used to look to repeat things...

"THE BEGIN OF MAYBE"

Where does maybe is my m
ism I
had a had-time maybe
I been had
been handed had-isms
been through wicked wickeds
been time to
to have a
a time to
maybe mine
maybe sick sick this was
body-had me a time
this body had me
in time I had seen
and I, m is my ism had kept on
I had kept this body at bay
a bad badness I had
I was wicked-sick with had
when will sick-wicked-with have me
will time have what I have when had-time had me
and maybe let
me body body was was had was I
her body was I
her body

"FRASSLE-DAY GOATS OR GODS"

I

Might my May I be everywhisp an' wanted you to be. An' thereby give me space to
sleep deep of dawn you. Take 2 cents of it—1 back—3 forward—Say May I? Might
Museicia carry my verbs on to unknown you an' me-lands...maybe, I am the right to
messiah's equilibrium. To her mighty brain or scrawny heart. To the left of her, threshes
the flap of coincidence. Rain to the angels is again my bible. And I live to capture
what I don't know. To put it into words and be the expert of what, exactly, it is, I
know nothing about. My very being depends on uncertainty, how can I put this so you
understand...I need to be stupid to continue this muddle, may I never know! May it
always be a caggle of toe-rut to play with and form castles of play-dust. May the princes
I imagine be equally inept and thereby keep me from ever imagining goals goats or
gods. May the ghouls I imagine when I fail at this be fumbling foogls who have no
goagls. My goal is to have no goals, so I fail immediately...ahhh...now we can start over.

Nurse the dark side, hummerbug. This urge torture to torture torture...it is what
brings them to separation. What busts the mind. Sussed and over. Fracked inna
kitch-dead. Pop is a mom—Bell Rang!—the Bell Rang!-the-the-Bell-that-that-Rang-
in-my-Head! (*there are Mondays in my Friday*)

Utilize the energy of evil to create, or just be, or own horsers of suburbia you couldn't
get before. If even we can only an' only be who we are. And I see what passes for
incognito was presented inna package-hole, appetizing, wet and easy. And this allows
you to look at pleasies in the world. Junk cars pile, spill the tracks, go away the fate
of escape. Filth words excaviched by thee, sire, "You aslike yourself into a mutual
warmering pool?" The Cache of Indignance, hazardous to polite. Stainless steel
forkhead, severed happy. Withdrawn. Insure-regard-in' his jock at her! She scoffs her
pits at 'im! He bodraggles pud! Like a real snot nose! She holds, in the air! (it goes
with going). Tight-ass grip lawn mower. Chainsaw Gimlet. Asian Armadillo wrestles
tongue with Maybelle Play-Doe, eyes as faun as flora. She knows mistakes come in
geysers to those who wait. M'man floats the gravy over gardunias. Licking restraint
over canals. Marrow presumes strangulation as we take steps our steps over steps we
take just we took just stepped on we steeped it did, over crabs curling Singer-Genies.
Crack my hands off, leave of absence, take me to the prize and bless the languag!

II

And stopped it on the steps, we did, where it's all an' all that. An' in that one beadless linger...the same. Only his wicked vitriol, drips salivat. The chain-up passals prey, on the villainous faraway—you. A you, a lace me, a whee, and a why; will all adorn covers, cere-money, the cash of Ceres' knees...lackluster spray pontoons tag the pair, the pair circle invite space. "The Only Thing Jittery Is My All, It Circles The Involve Of Space." Involve Space. Tied by the tongue. Falls from the mouth. A marker to journey. A spike to rage. Scrape the scritch of words... my survival depends on this world. My fate perhaps sharpened by tongue. (*it's just THIS part of Friday feels like Monday*)

All tense and scraggled. A fit comfort far things and faere rarist things shaggered. Today leaves a lot to be, thee sire. And a lot to be, thee sire...accepts it. You know a Moggleday, she's happy somewhere that finally, she makes it into someone's Frassleday! Right! Oh That's Razzle! For a real...whizzer! OAHU-AHA...doesn't the Sayer crawl alongingly! Blithely have you AVE-NEW! It is the show-up of a fellow Palmo, the dear of felicitous win-someone-y, sameasone...ony-onna-honey, that involves the space they're in. The pass of sin. THE WEEKLY WIGGLE BEGINS:

III

Niger is a short back, followed by two islands in low-cut ignorance.
 MC Faux Beret/Bay Feuraux/Mocha Tote/Karaoke Kafka/Carry/Jocka-
  Moatee-Goat...Nasty.
   Luna Kovsky/Coughs aLotski. Poseur smoke...
    Ladders the ceiling. Open Peeling. Pope-On-A-Dope...
     Throats a rrrrroatal E-mote from the folkes...
      "A Vocal Odal To Fingertip Podal".
Apollo... A-poistes himself expectantly.
 Pigleopatra piddles her *pinchon*.
  Ahhh, machine...the full package!
   THESE are the kind of Fridays that don't-
    NEED are the kind of Mondays that don't-
     BELONG in the kind of Fridays that THESE are!

Light your Vaticandles, PO-ESSI-PO-EPPY...

    The Papal-eoples are o-PO-os-SI-tives of an ES-presso happening!

        Creme de la EX-cremente, please.

            Oh...you changed your name from 3 wheels ago?

                3-week Abysinnia? New names new shields new

                    3-year pectorals.

Blueist of all rotate.

    She rotates the ceiling in finite Warzawa infinit.

        Tumult Grace. Parcel to sin. Spokes of jute. Now. The.

                          SCREEEEECH...SCREEEEECH...

            Soar, Compose, Grin, Guide...

        Churn, Mecano, Mico, Hold...

SCREEEEECH...SCREEEEECH...

An' it turns, this way, an' once turned that, way back to revol, to tute, steppes-A.Z.-to-peeks. Tu-pids don't get it! Soar, the daddy form...so many travels along the way. Gain, Grin, Cha, Chagrin...Maddy O Moggleday...Zip it:

    I hear the air goes out for coffee when she's lovely.

        I really see I would explode t'were I th' wincer.

            I fear a ferret is a fugue in spirit pincers.

                So I may win, sir! What goes around, sir... What goes around!

IV

And how it drips everything, your ears. And how the expected rhythm numbs. And how THAT does not climb, but rather puts O's-an-Origs-an-I's-an-Inals...into the sieve. Splinters a person. Ali. Ty. To A. an' G. is a I.D. is O.D. down wit G?..OH That Rizzles! How people leave their people at the door an' dear the not-people people at the their. A. Py. is what that. is. A goodness thing numbing if even the repetition of badness is a numbing thing. Aslant of say-hello. I play my life, expert of as you are. And you can stay the change. Master the same way. (repetition). Conform to what you don't know. Offend your own personality. Dear Raggle Looner, grow wingats an' become the little ing-gnat you always wanted to lap at. gnlap. a gnat. yr lap. s'a pap spat to slap at, WHAP!

So, many pretty girls, pretty semblances to many boys. So, many pretty boys, and in replacement...a fast for all sin. The surface plays under the shine. Razzle, might I kiss 'em an' blow the Booty Out?! NO to that one only an' only when I NO when I no-no-never see the day now. (much of it). Never seal the stars. My pocket filled of change. Never give the rain now. May I never know the wrong-day hello (*just this part only when I fall, feels like that part only*). My FLAWS they seem to my GET, to get one, so might my attrition be so calculated, as to include YOU in my wishes? Oh Bella BetPhaBetla, most weekday whisprells slant the says of say-hello speakday ...you...*WHAP!*..the man who wears ivory for a shirt isn't night, he only lost indigo-night-line in the wash. Sink in the bathe of Involve Space, strailing in sud-udden years.

C.M.K.Y.-R.G.D-FOCOLTRON-SAM-EP.P.P.O.O-C.O.N.-VERSI-VOUS-TO-PRO-KEDS!

April was my month of Tuesdays.
    My spum. My acorn.
        My effectual scrootch lays grinning, bejewelled of circumference.
            Severance...Get These Mondays Out Of My Friday!!!...

SCREEEEECH...SCREEEEECH...Mofo-Sax another White-Boy into Bang-Land Dead by Hifi...SCREEEEECH...SCREEEEECH...Quarkerelle: the Moggleoon all Frassleoons are wary of...FREEEEEECH...SPREEEEECH...

Lily pads pink
    the nose browns, green
        to yellow masted stink.
            As the funnel routes:
                As the gain implutes:
                    As space invites the sloth-pierced height:
                        As might might be: Asly of me:
                            As required for rancid take-over:
                              (*eight days told*)

TURKON-TURRO...the cycle reveals itself to be a wheel of raincote Mondays locked in the whistle of Millifluent Fridays.

V

-Mummy...there a god? -Don't know...but there a goat!

What goats around goats around—insteading the point to go around. There...below
the chins, why it looks like the dear-people pack a wallop. I see...and it grows from
the bottom of your tongue? Hmmm, around the mouth an' cheeks...shavery, creech,
fine. Crack my face off, leave it bare...but let it get that bottom-of-the-tongue-
pierced-through-the-chin Look. The Real rakkles into the skin...don't it? BAHHHH-
HHH! Oh...Listen to rub belly dew. Blind and far behind. Oh...Help thee sire instill
shimmer tags. Take me to glassy eyes. "Once and Derriere," everybody said. Apollo
with his mouth of Tuesday. Juna rizzling her sun-says. The quills to the Gripot left
along the divide. Sit my review. So few. I hand you this and you swallow it whole.
The purge carries sensacious sizzle. This, the malestrom of Mako Swans...creasles a
look at you. Sit on the night, I live the eye of moonstorms. Float waterhard
slivery and milk. Came here. So here. And I awaiting for flight. Bent by the sloss of
magnificent blight. Freeze mite. Float lucid flowery T. And I color the shout...
Amarindo! Amarindo! Amarindo! Amarindo!

(epiloG'UE)

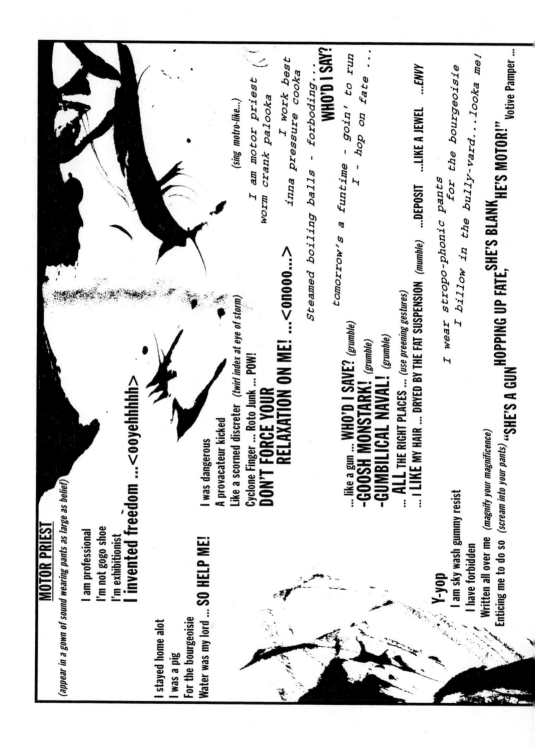

MOTOR PRIEST

(appear in a gown of sound wearing pants as large as belief)

I am professional
I'm not gogo shoe
I'm exhibitionist
I invented freedom ...<ooyehhhhh>

I stayed home alot
I was a pig
For the bourgeoisie
Water was my lord ... SO HELP ME!

I was dangerous
A provacateur kicked
Like a scorned discreter (twirl index at eye of storm)
Cyclone Finger ... Roto Junk ... POW!
DON'T FORCE YOUR
RELAXATION ON ME! ...<ohooo...>

(sing motro-like...)
I am motor priest
worm crank palooka
I work best
inna pressure cooka
Steamed boiling balls - forboding...
WHO'D I SAY?
tomorrow's a funtime - goin' to run
I - hop on fate ...

... like a gun ... WHO'D I SAVE? (grumble)
-GOOSH MONSTARK! (grumble)
-GUMBILICAL NAVAL! (grumble)
... ALL the RIGHT PLACES ... (use preening gestures)
... I LIKE MY HAIR ... DRYED BY THE FAT SUSPENSION (mumble) ...DEPOSIT ...LIKE A JEWEL ...ENVY

Y-yop

I am sky wash gummy resist
I have forbidden
Written all over me (magnify your magnificence)
Enticing me to do so (scream into your pants) "SHE'S A GUN HOPPING UP FATE, SHE'S BLANK HE'S MOTOR!" Votive Pamper ...

I wear stropo-phonic pants
for the bourgeoisie
I billow in the bully-vard...looka me!

... **ROTRO PUMP!** I give you destiny ... you jump!

Why don't you give ME destiny?
Like bald needle in silver sky
Like gutter snipe gotten ripe ... might you ... **SHINE, SHAPELESS HUFF!**
(scream to the heavens) **BINGO NIHILIST!**
<ohnooo....>
WHAT SAY, INFINITUMMY
GOT THE HUMP! WATTA BOOR!

My trousers worn inside Out round where I'm NOT LOOK A' ME, POPS! **GUMBOT SARIAH'S GOT THE CHOPS!**

I was a blank jab A fingerprint faceless Ego funk ... IT'S ONLY ID IF YOUR CHAD GROPS! SEE ... SHE IS BOOT! I MEAN ...

(oh, help me horn my hoofed potential)
help me horn my hoofed potential

I was a star in a cave
Where rocks meet
Realizing victory
As a package of lies
I was replaced ... < JERK FROUFROU! nyeee> They said - my morals were goofy ... **MOTOR PUS, BABY!**
I GOT SHOT!

(open palm gesture between crotch and imaginary used car)

I was a windsock
Ragging the world
With inertia poodles
Unconditional
I am ... Professional
I have ... no identification

SEPERATIST INVASION

There have been a thousand sightings
of people I used to know.
Separations of copies of
who it is they look like, backed up
by carbons of who they are.

In hornrim disruption
our spaceship fires up past zero.
The concert has happened
and all these people of me,
have still to go home.

Who it is that knows me
is who I went to school with,
but I've graduated
and all the words we sing—now
I'm here, sugar in my hand

searching for your face.

WHATWHATWHAT

•

N O W

- I gonna lick you *ss!
- the whole ess? or jess the hole?
- *sshole!

bycyclee
duplette triplet
beasta-clette salute!
the troops have begun

the sag
the hefted tent
the crotchball
tongueing up the grunt, alors!
in my favorite arms...I hold a once-a-day dooya-dooya

- don't the Don't have a right
  to who-ity?...anon
- whassup with all that
  hup-hup-tuity?

bycyclee dulce
trycyclee who-say
anon
again
alors...

- !MOUNTAINANT!

a malaise dolor
neatly braided rows alouette

- I gonna lick you...

at the yes of all
sags the finish

- the whole? or jest the...
- s hole!

as I hold tight .
in my favorite one day meadow
the sky plummets in my arms

& TO THE AUDIENCE

Truly - Odorous
Trudy - Odeant
Olee - Iffious
Onor - Underant
Effy - Idiot
Instal - Impotent
Nozzle - Newt
Dimple - Dent
Coolee
De - Koois : 2 - 3...?
...DA!

GELAPAGOS

Give the lovely Mrs. Fojetes my warmth THAT MAY
PROVE STICKY You can handle it —
Droopy Wafer was a cracker hack'er offly THAT MAY
PROVE STICKLY You can wrangle it —
Hick'er up and handle simply SHE MAY LIMPLY
ASK FOR JOVE Then give her Job or Jibe or
Solomon The Juice CONCUBUSTIER Once a recluse
NOW A PARA-DEUCIER You can sing a bit—
Slip a nip into the nanny raze a rip & roil it
stiffly quite politely CUT THE MONGOLOOKIE
MAYBE Might you then but please—
Give the lovely Miss Tor-esticles
my best-tickles

here's what happens

got sick
calls the blood-house
says
cousin you ain't no better
(them to me)...than a sanctimonkio savior
seekin' sacrilligid saturns
sassafrass-alatin' soup rings
said

SAY HOME-BRE...
why you GETS
that GOT again?

so here's what happens

got sicker
calls b-home (sayin)

SAY CUZ...
ain't the better to lay
and take the bed to
wet you by?

say I'm sayin'

sees wha's happens
gets the tonic
chronic
deep
twice
you GOT it
later

OARS

No row built on mirror ships
No hard boiled sticks
No harmony hits into the head
The weapon for change - directions of time

Flaps welded by shatter
No push on a babble
No made up come-onia
Towering over
No Torres

A Spain of PoMo times
In cloaks of No
In blinds of Madrigal
Constellating by the bay
In all the same ways

Curtain to lake
Am I
My hands pass
Through
Night veils
No
Smudgy pap draggin'
No 'nother drift

And all the same
At times ignored
As if
I didn't existed

TOUR la BETTE EPOCH de MONTREPID-UTIAE

By licorice kisses-
      crullers unwinding, hug by hug...✕...◯
By Yakitude Bay-
      the parallel breeze orbiting, a cast-off weem, a no-rounda GO-GO...✕...◯
By gutted mirrors, he stands...HOT SHITAKE!

suckle - nut

nickle - grunt

sickle - wick

change of spurt

shift-back

kick - pick

      ...one by one the 6th gear comes...✕...◯

Already...little squirts line up & claim victory roses-
a kiss of the lovely Mongoleena's razor warmth on my cheek.
By light of mellow winter's equine.
By the blueyellow maze of a thin grunt, a tall finish - all
on the line, he stands...in New Wean GELAPO-GOP!
        a pop
           cilia - simp
            stink - O - tang
            orang - A - roly
        licorice man...nobbling on the haze.

     Round with sugary arms
    dripping powdered dipper songs.
    In the haze, he waves us on
      from a clock environs, to a dark one - GO!
        Donut Sandanista
          cycles past the feast...uh!
                | ad lib mambo riff |

Graze on
Ground
Grinder
Mountaineers -
Central
Daylight
of Gears - POP!

| quick change of tires | - STOP!
| inner eimer weaned tuby weemer - was to be | - GO!

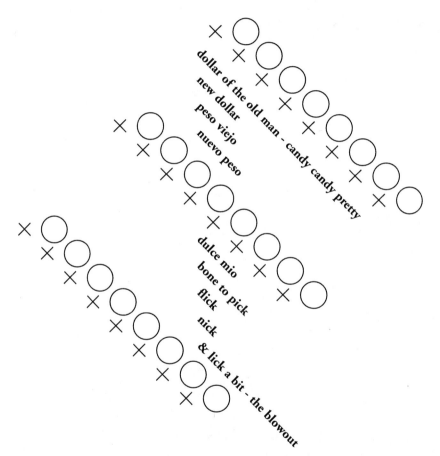

dollar of the old man - candy candy pretty
new dollar
peso viejo
nuevo peso

dulce mio
bone to pick
flick
nick
& lick a bit - the blowout

baby's   she
gotta   uses to
hardon   replace

my head   shit
with that   never goes
the head that   to waste

she never   never
sees the   never
light of the   day

til bay-bay say: HEY-HEY
                            I gotta use the
                        BOM-BOMB
                            I bang you head with
                        THAT-ONE
                            They looka alla
                        SAME-O
                        THAT-THAT-ONE
                        YEH-YAY-O
                            Now Mamone Fishois
                        PLAY

I boing   I twang it
you little   witta
eyeball   chaser see

baby's   that never
gotta   goes to
hardon   waste-ugh!
                    ⌐ ad lib samba riff ¬

45

THE RIME OF THE DONUT KING

World leaders choose
what they want to call their world
The sol-pow of another ray

In say-so time
they rule
    color
    strain
    &
    punch
    into another shape...another day

PLAY-DOH PLANETS

It's easy to guide a little shapeless one
as the thing you hold up & look through
the thing you eat, my pretty donut...

everything I am, is in my holes

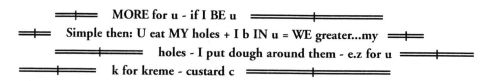

MORE for u - if I BE u
Simple then: U eat MY holes + I b IN u = WE greater...my
holes - I put dough around them - e.z for u
k for kreme - custard c

theroundofthingsIvebeenthinkingabout there...

...in every think
    ...u dunk
        ...my wonder

To go, a dozen - behind
my back - crullers, in loop time...I see

thisbelt
theonetoomanyholeofit

...falling

throughmycrown

my arms powdered in a coated dream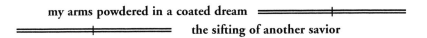
the sifting of another savior

Holes
have begun to appear...

●

to talk to themselves into help from other holes
to DONT DUNK US AGAIN!
to the whole s? or just a gathering of holes
to form the one great world A WHOLE BOX - of

Holes
in halo formation
have begun to appear...   glazed

frosted

twisted

SCENE 9 : RETRO

AMMA-NAMMA-NO
AMMA-NAMMA-NO   WHOAH
    thassa rancid answer
    for a HEY-HEY!
YO-YO,
Little BO'S barkin' up his doobie, again!
    A butt-woofer? is he...
    my, doesn't THAT smack of
    regionalism!
Of local pamperism!
    Of MisterWimple squeezinism!

⟹   Howya gonna
⟹   RUMPLE UP a keep - an' kees em
⟹   down
⟹   on the farm,
⟹   after the cous cous
⟹   big dip's
⟹   a runny sop-diape?
⟹ ⟹ ⟹ a soggy biscuit? cuz?

A doo rant - HOWYA - to ya!
And to yer quest for the truth?
I am - respect for yer - romance...

But that boomboom
bellybutton's on the wrong
TUM-TA-TUM-TUM!

        ↑   ↑   ↑   ↑

PUSHIN' ALONG
PUSHIN' ALONG
PUSHIN' ALONG...YA GO BOOM

SILENCE & SEEING

and if you claim solace
at a distance
from what you know

and if that one embrace
knows too well
what comes with solace

silence & seeing

and if that claim
might come translucent
in image & faith

and passage of skin
so air in promise
so placed in distance

and if that one embrace
of distance
passes distance placed

and if then
befriends the line
its make

what knows too well
what breaks

and if you claim
if and then
as friend

CLOCKTION

>>> The Waistcoat for Revolution
has slipped below the knees
⌜ just in time ⌟ How easy...this tragedy
          how tragically easy...this morning of ASS:

tempest   *lust*   *fluttercuts*

Cold from the clothed butt...WATCH OUT!
TOU-CHALO!
TOUCHÉ-LO!
TOUCHEE-IT!

TOUCH IT!

     ...the clockman, he watches you
              WaWaWaitaminute!

>>> The Occasional Skirt
has swiped against an ocean of ASS: ...something, huh?
        how I keep going back and forth on "it"
How easy...to sell time in a cooler - dripping
       one year at a time
Thirsty for another hour - WITH A FACE LIKE THAT?

                You ⎯
              ⎡ ARE
             interested ⎦
>>>The Droppers of Liberation   ⎣ in
worn by the foot - first left - then...He watches you
          wawawater,
        He...uh, watching   huh? ⎯
     Heya Watcher
         Hiya Hiya Water Watha
    Clock-t'yeh
       Caught-t'yah

BEAUTY FART

O...
I Heart I   ...as a girl of infinite direction

O...
I Hear I   ...as beauty mark is my pupil

anon
again
alors...repetez:

"Jay - Sweez - French - Neempphhh..." ...fete!

I n your snore of 7 seconds
I hear all of Mother Russia escaping.
Mother of sand.
I wanna clean up the table
Mother may I?
...wanna drop a bundle

adonde
adundle
abondanza...REPETEZ:

"I Wanna Do The %#!@ Homeboy Dance On His Face!"*

O...
I
I
I yaawwn

51

...as a mouth of India, lips of soil
...as a girl of intrigue, ruby secrets
...as I rub
  I heart
  I dance as a beauty mark
  on the face of the world

✳

O...
Who Hearts I

INQUISITE EVENING

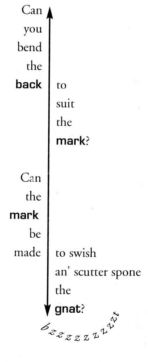

Can
you
bend
the
back | to
suit
the
mark?

Can
the
mark
be
made | to swish
an' scutter spone
the
gnat?
bzzzzzzzzzt

Would
"punctu"
punch you-udy
out? | Unctuate
the
booty? (the booty)

bzzzzzzzzzt (tabouli?)

Is
a
did
down
there | nary
a
done? (a pary)

hary...
cAry...
XARY...!?

...oh nothing!
(having done it in the back)

A **happ** is **appening** downstage,
Exclam - BANG - turn around!
It is the **back** that is it, has
the **whole** why - part
of **who**.

I've done to me...nothing.
I step on you, period.
Proundly you sit! (croundly) _1zzzzzzzzzq_

I'm Off!
(I'm off...i'm off...)...the **offals** of inquisite evening to you.
For I have a balloon tie, a helium noose
where I hang the truth.

I'S HOLE

a WAIT! w e n t

I want for the holes to break   i
I wait for the holes to speak   n | to sin a proper sin |

I'm... ...sort of... ...waiting... ...for the... ...holes... ...to... ...speak...

There's a bit of the map about you,
you're a wisher...aren't you? ...a journey scarred...
Is one fall, followed by repetition?
Aye, by proper sin (one)...and
Mama Fishy.

Mamone Fishoisé
nets sh'flights of wet 'lectric click 'eels.
The Think:
to SHOULD the MAKE of them...THAT is sin.
Flying the bodyscape - the transcope
of the ONLY you've dreamnt of.

That's it...You're a Bed-Wetter!
Who's the fishy?
Who coos a dishy bit?
A do-er?
A who?
A who-er?
A coo-coo-coo-er?   I think
you fall into what you know,
...the right way to sin?
to have Mama show you
...the right way to sin!
to unlock your Holy Brazil.
to scrape your hill.
to make your hole.

A PROPER SEED

there is a time often discovered...
it is after life...maybe,
it is often life...maybe,
it is a should I—
but my mom was only the holder...

should I dissipate the revolutions...
should I time often...
should I very clear of eyeballs...
should I diminish...
should I lengthen copper radiant...
should I should at all...
                sometimes i feel
                sometimes i mind
                sometimes i feel like i'm losing my mind

                hear me my child
                as i breathe my child
                feel me in you as my mind goes wild

should I seive the daily hour...
should I long and prosper...
                an' all they do is call his number
do you like Ring-o-lievio...
a noisy thing, o-leivio...
should I speak...
should I dunk / styrate - soar the island...
(powder the question)...do you like me?

a dead hold—a scold of tongue—a maybe spot—a wet one...
a donut on sandy knees...
the proper seed...
                if i live so strong
                can i die so strong
                can it be that you were my life all along

THE EMPEROR'S NEW ROBE

Color of death is coincidence, but love is realistic.
The painting of Okay highlights, in style, good what's done—
like now, what we do with other things.
Like a profile of what's out of reach—a nose
or someone's breast. Like that's how you flower
the opposition, floor! Palimpset of buggery, tracing page
invisible skin—our other thing.

Like then—the catch of when. They greet you
put a belt of arm around your ass, or someone's tulip
significant meaning to the stamen—don't belong to you.
What did you do with that what!
What did YOU do with THAT what!
What did you do with that, what?

Don't touch—no other thing, WHAT
isn't yours. Even if it's soft, especially if it's soft, even
if it's curvy, especially, how about something
soft and curvy, tasty and licky?
Because I'm not. Would you want that?

You touch what you're NOT?
Touching nots, becomes one is,
a large one that comes from not—like this...
is nowhere.

Attached to nowhere—to the reverse side
of invisible, so to say, what sees behind.
I still something.

Trade this burn—the part of your position
recognized by nothing.
Cheers to the lousy and all their laundry
attached to nowhere—wearing expensive nothing.

in
an
argument
of
kings

with
each
as
equal
as
each

which
one
delivers
flowers
on
death
day

which
one
kills
promises

A BUILDING OF VOICE

the Bldg is calm
a host of voice
is outside—
in an
unBldg of people
we are unvoiced

inside
purses coats & unthings
gather—
waiting for their people
people's things
waiting for people to return

empty people
full of empty
unpeopled—
of ground of sound of
center
walk around

find your
person's people your finding's
voice—
walk around &
empty out your Bldg
un, all over again, if you want

the Bldg is calm
it is the voice
that is peopled

BONE BOY

come upon a family, eating dinner
outdoors, their frontyard has no walls
right in street, they've set up
table with umbrella, rain has just happened

slippery cobblestreets, wet with danger
come upon a boy with olive skin, black hair
deep black eyes, he sees me, quickly
puts white something in his jet black hair

red t-shirt, yellow shorts at dinner table,
he is jester for family dinner, mom and pop
in t-shirts, sit back, laugh as he adjusts
item placed in hair, air smells, combo of

fresh rain and freshly smoked fish, smoky
rain, delicious herbs and fresh wine, rain
paints olive picture of street, polished stone, boy's
hairpiece looks like bone of something, or like

strange brush, or comb, or bonecomb of octopi-whale,
or swordfish lung, or angelhair macaroon, or like
clipped bowtie cuttlefish, or squid bleached by mom
in vat of boiling smoke, or croatian guppy mutate, or

javanese man o'war skeleto-fings, or wrongway pirahna snatch, or
poontang of boned barge, or hairpiece of bonedad, or clipped
soccer match on radio fuzz, or afternoon jewel, or big-eyed
bangle bush, or storm-hand skelt-ray, or entire eagle claw

bleached by boiling mom, or basilica for miniature sainthood, or
bone of halo gripping black inferno head of moon-child, or
blinded eclipse passing over innocent traitor, or
slaughter of fresco fromp uncovered after years of marinara

and risotto, or just cheap bowtie clip, or perhaps white plastic nature
on black seahead, or wide-eyed innocent exchange rate, or mispronounced
genitalia for summer blondes of he's and she's, or an archipelago of lynch-mobs,
or mow-fat tombo, or little girl's black lace skeleton martyred by her death wheel, or

a stone of sainthood etched by miscreant little tykes, or 3 beauty boys
adolescent smokers onna train of ideals, or bone of pubes split by an ocean of smoke,
or bridge between eyebrows, or sun's eyebrow chunked by rat bastard moon
burping pink sky, or silver adriatic, or watergreen hydrofoil on circular birdbones

migrating over a sailor's stomach gutted by years of roiling waves, or
a knapsack's bone clenched onna velvet poor-boy, or perhaps it's a distant city
of white bone onna black-hair hilltop built around natural locks, or maybe
seal-bone etched by storyteller's tongue, or perhaps whalebone

fetched by a cloudy dog, or a ribbon of light painting itself across horizon,
or skystorm passing black to white as separation offers surrender
its rain to torment, or torrential skeleton-typhoon pouring down manuscripts
illuminated by franciscan monks on fire, or avenues of stone monoliths

catching sun's shadow to form directional traffic lights for nation of people
buried under years of polished stone, or street; bone-white on black soil
rich with daylight, or labyrinth of marrow filled by family dinner, or
a father and mother cooking fresh bone fish, handing little boy

bone to play with, after boiling fresh bone,
laughing at bone-boy, inserting bone in hair,
freshly boned bone-boy, onna street, or a frontyard
without walls, with an olive boy, in red and yellow,

wearing something white in his black hair,
holding his hands, very tight, gazing
with jet black eyes, waiting,
for someone like me to pass by, and notice

CANYON SUITE

•

A PARALLEL TEXT
IN FIVE PARTS

I

CNN **effen**-enters
therein; MoFo
bleeps the leap into deep.   *"...Do I*
                                                stare, or
                                          talk to you?..."

A Moaning Beat-Moron
                    S.O.B.
drowns tomorrows
                         drowns a Beep
by the wings.
                         a world away.

eMeffen **Beat World**...
third eye of the sun.   *"...Such*
                                          lovely moons
                          in your moan, my dear!..."

                    (issa He-world,
                    a who?)
She?   *"...He?"*
                    Who?

                    "...ooooooh...see how nice and
                         clean the floor looks?..."
                    (snap)
                                          "SEE !

HOW !   *NICE ! AND !*

CLEAN ! THE !   *FLOOR ! LOOKS !"*
                    (snap)

See, I never look down.

See, I see and then again...   *"...anon..."*

there...she isn't,

SNAP! BLEEP!

effen is,

                              "...See...N N..."

there she is!,

A bleak world

sore of end.

                    "...Anon.i.me,...quwherrrr isst
                              my rentured slave?..."

EFFIT!

My

Beat slave, **N**

then denters.   *"...O Sure, renting*
                    a fencing instructor?...
                              enter then!"

see **He**...

then **She**...

                    bleak of enter...

will **then** (cnn),

LEEEEEEEEEEP into deep.

She: *"...& I*
                    stare at the world
                    in my mirror,

& every day   *is tomorrow,*

                                          & I

stare   *at tomorrow,*

                                            & my

world   *wants to end,*

                                            & I

drown   *what I seek,*

                                            & I

            want to complete this

reach

                                         reach

the world for tomorrow..."

(Wretched *Effer*)

Bite Bleeply

under

MoFo there...   *"...Where...?"*

                         BLEEEEEEEEEEP!!!

Bite

what I slave for

else...

I go,

I die,

am now nothing, but...   *"...bleep..."*

*   *   *   *   *   *   *

II

Span C.

-SI???

Pan.

-Y...CANTA?

Si.

-Y...M?

T.V!

-SI???

Z.

-Y...MATTA?

Uno.

-SI???

Un Hundred.

-ISH?

B!

-C???

Nappa.

-PAN?

(SHHHHH!!!!!)

-sssspan...?

Si.

-SI???

Ola.

-ELLO?

Yo Soy.

-SI?

I Be!

(timbre)

(timbre)

(timbre)

-ELLO?

L.I.B.

* * * * * *

III

"WHERE THE WHERE?
*WHEN T**HE***
 * **THEN?***
*LE**AP**Ed THE*
    BLEEP!...
J'ACCUSE!!!!!"

We open at the crux herein;
Axis-Kala Yori,
(relation to Mecca BC: Unknown)
The m**asses**
have blindly accused
the **Lovely-Face Children**
of sight-robbing the populace.

In worldgear silk of night
c**her**ry tombstone m**ono**cle
in hand
...Sappilow Kinsman
rephrases the question:

  *"w**HERE** WERE YOU*
       WHEN SHE
 *WAS T**HERE?"***

Taken aback by such
bum-rush attactics...
Winslow Concubus, tattler
of tiger tail, attempts
deflection through seduction:

"...HeeeeeeaaaaaaHeeHaa!
You've gotta lovely..."

"MY FACE!"

"...Aha! You like 'em! My legs!..."

"MY DRESS!"

Win**slow** Concu**bus,**
Lovely-Face Child of Mecca B.C....
(*SI, M . E . C . C.*
A . B . C .) saunters, approachably,
towards
s**A**p**pillow** Kins**man**'s
ruby-throated **closet.**

"...Your shirt, your tie?..."

"Shoopy!"
Weary of canary sigh,
            "Shoopy!"
mirror of tomorrow...she
            "Shy!"
drowns the day...as she
            "Shy!"
enters the closet.

Underwear one hand
linger herself the other.

Quiet
in the ruby-dark
she...
closes the door.

Alone.
Disrobed.
Waiting.   *"...shhhh !..."*

                    "MY APARTMENT?"
Sappilow Kinsman
was confused.

Traveled to Asia, said:
                    "THE BEDROOM?"
                              "...AHA!..."
Traveled to Africa, said:
                    "THE KITCHEN?"
                              "...AHA!..."
Traveled to Antarctica, said:
                    "THE BATHROOM?"
                              "...AHA!..."

SHHHH!

We close at the place
accused of the world.

A blindly, bleeply enter...
where hers is his and his
is hers.

* * * * * * *

IV

"...-C???..."

Span!

Corner span,
from every world Beat.

*"...Isn't there
a who I'm looking for?..."*

**You've got such
a lovely moan, my dear!**

That span of time
reckless to the moon...bites
the night, Beat slave,
with ruby dentures.

*"...b...
...b...
...beat slave..."*

A span of lies across tomorrow,
and frankly...

Invisitude to nightling!

*"Volitude...might wing
span the silk of night?"*

Once a 'morrow, a time to C.

SI???

'ELLO???

Little corners of brightness
blur *surround*...yet
live to give...and
leap...and go.

ELO???

My glass,
the canyon I peer through.
My every corner.

'LO???

He:

"Do I, talking to you, who aren't here?"

She:

"Do I stare off into deep C?"

He:

"Amma think about it."

She:

"Amma check your messages.

Amma lookit the floor.

Amma never look down!"

He:

"Dark book of balance."

She:

"Amma bite too deep?"

He:

"Look, you...

Bleeeeeeeeeeep!!!!!

We pan to a moment, waiting for blur.

"Silver-Throated Mom!"

A **moron** drowns clock-ticks
back, a day ago...where my day sits...
A '**morrow** dips in sleep.

He: *"& I saw that many days*

fell out,

                              & I look

at you and see

something I've found,

                              & I don't

know what it is

I'm looking for,

                              & I know

I found something

when I found you,

                              & I pulled

my skin, sky-taut."

She: *"Copper-Plated Pop!"*

* * * * * * *

V

A Friendly Next,
by Mary Van Many...sings a lark
in Coral Gables.

He: *"Frankly my dear..."*   She...

sings a seeming song,
sings seems...like she's here.

*"Her **here is** Her"*

Seems,
she's got it worked out.
Seems,
she's got it together.

Mary Van Many, larking
a seeming song...
Seems to have found her reach.
(snap)
Her wings...stretched
Her arms...stretched-shattered...
"...she-seems..."
(snap)
Ready to take off
Like she's   *"...she's..."*
never taken off before.   *"...never..."*
                                    "...before..."

Seems like her wing span
is the world.
Too big for the world.

Seems her span

                                     is the world.

              (snap)

Beat

                                      the world.

              (snap)

SEEMS

She's stretching her reach...

                    she's never before, like

She's never Before,

              She's

Stretching ***Before***

into ***More***...into'Morrows...

Stretching

              (snap)

She's

Stretching

                    (snap)

She's

Breaking

                        (snap)

She's stretching

                          (snap)

            SEEMS

She's

RipRipping her   *her*

                  days

day

into   *into*

many days   *days*

Mary
Van
Many,
Lark
To any

Mark-Harry-Dick, Rips   *Her day*

> *Her many days*
> *Rip*
> *Her world Rips*
> *Her wing span*
> *Breaks*
> *Her*
> *Takes*
> *Off*
> *Breaks the day*
> *Sees the world*
> *She's the world*
> *Span*
> *C Span*
> *Span...si*

-finalto-

* * * * * * *

75

A MAN OF TWO

A man whose face has begun to fall into itself
       is a man who has lived
A man whose face has begun to congeal into itself
       is a man who has lived
A man whose face has begun to become into itself
       is a man who wears his life
A man who shows his face turning into itself
       is a man who has bitten the fruits off his life
A man who's truly faced his fruits
       is a man who has developed a taste for life
A man whose cheekbones are higher than his nose and protrude forward
out of his eyesockets beyond his eyelashes
       is a man I would like to meet
A man who laughs through the squint of his eye at life's abnormal normality
       is a man who one day I would hope to become
A man with a face so tanned by life's vulgar wrinkalities that his teeth have met his ears
on their way toward his knuckles in a jovial slap to life's bitter jokeries
       is a man I have seen
       and wished to have shook his bony hand
       while slapping his concaved back enroute to herniated nobility
       as life's bitter torment has greased the championed butt of its wean
       over his by now completely caved-in featureless face with nubs
       appearing as buds on a newly migrated podface wearing
       a freshly pressed blue shirt is a man who laughs at life's incredible irony
       while whoring his pride
       a man I would one day hope to have unearthed at peacetime
       a man I would time myself with
       tie myself to
       myself in two
A man in two
       is a man with no face
       a man who has lived
A man who has begun to become itself
       is a man who has lived

THE ENERGY OF MATTER ACCELERATED

Combine Plato No. 3 with Plato No. 4;
Spend a combination of 2 prices on combined plates;
Order the menu, combine the tip with the rent; and offer a compromise;
Combine Freud No. 2 with Roosevelts 3, 4 & 9;
Pavlov visiting Pavlov understands the nude inclination;
Hegel No. 7 levels Hegels No. 8 thru 50;
The combined root of despair lies in Seuss; No.'s 18, 20 & 63;
Brave meat; boiled front; Nikolai's naught pence wrought's asylum;
Enjoy Coffee with Steamed Milk No.'s 80 thru 82;
Combine the eggs from Plate Sister Suze with an omelette of water;
A Bear who is dangerous will wave goodbye 13 times;
A No. 2 Bear will merely pretend;
Aristotle combines Boris No. 3 with Yeltsin No. 42 wearing Bear No. 14 as a toga;
3 DaVinci's from France drink bad Yoohoo; Viral Infections No. 30 thru 60 wait;
Strong Pipas; wait; Strong Pipas; wait;
Quarrel with a Spanish Demon who claims liberation; then; prepare for prophecy;
Franco No. 4 wears the bloodied shirt of France No. 2;
No. 1 has no face but combines the shoes & nose of Nixons 8 & 70;
With the ears, wit & eyebrow of Hepburns 3, 4 & 59;
Will Smiths No. 17 & 18 are in cahoots with Edison...the only one of him is him;
Coca Cola 3,659,725 & No. 2; settle final debts as:
Marching bands from High Schools 56 & 839; teach a complicated bossa nova rhythm;
To the senior citizens from Titanic 74 & Sartre 1;
Fiefdom of mountain sultan 30 numbers 90 among his warlords;
Cappucin Monkeys No. 64 thru 87 perfect their ammunition;
While marching to cornet bandoleer No. 4; whose mothers 5 & 7 challenged NASA;
By controling Nietschke No. 3,800 combined with Voltaires No. 7 & 16;
There is jazz in Marseille No. 2; a festival in No. 5; and 14 Bibles for the remaining flood;
Olga Sympathy calls for Non Di Vida; counting on 7 hands;
The loves of a frozen clock; a land struck seasong; and No. 3 Simpson's guilty haircut;

> *that is*—a gas station
> called—*that is*
> *esso*—or just—*that*
> the *that* tiger—frosted gas
> station—of *thats*

Evening No. 38 borrows twilight from No. 39;

Dinner finds its way down proper channels;

Evening No. 37 is the perfect one; and appears naked; in a dream;

Of daylights 8, 65, 14, 8,639, 25, 552, 77, 12, 43, 16, 257, 247, 246, 38,092 & 11;

They all fight the tide of history; while 3 men in a hut warn the village;

By sending a donkey to Capital City;

Warhols 4 & 17 complete completely; taking a nap in siestas 4 & 5;

The remaining images fall as a shirt; worn by the combined star power;

Of Charlton Heston No. 16 & Brad Pitts 49 thru 138;

Gregory Peck No.s 1 & 4 accept the Oscar for Boys Of Brazil Pt. II;

Warring with each other's fiefdoms; a scar of mountains across their ancient faces;

Williamson Hitchcock; now 3; combines the knuckled foreheads of;

Sister Sledge in the marketplace; & gives away fresh bowls of soup;

To whomever is good at math; Puff Adders 21 & 7 coil up;

As Charmer No. 25 answers the daylight mask with sways of smoke;

From the head of Disney No. 7; who bubble wraps Disneys 6 thru 60;

While fingering the debut of Madonna No. 3; Beckett No. 12 floats on Atlantic Lake;

Enticing Pacific No. 7 with a shanty from borrowed youth; Oh

> rip the night oil well, Oh
>
> pour this exceeda, Oh
>
> flip the bright city, With
>
> weeders dear reader, Oh
>
> pollute my extruder, My
>
> hills are much nuder, Ah
>
> well there's a flashlight, Ah
>
> hell it's earth's fool;

Mousal no twertal wins the race; comes in fastal not fertile;

Tyson Squared clobbers Givens Infinity;

Perils from dry heat; Frida Kahlo is a sore loser;

Defends the honor of Andre Breton 18, 42 & 6; traveling in a loud shirt;

The American shows some leg; Didac No. 2 steals a yawn from Sandman;

Converts it to sonic boom; murdered by street of jazz; illumination cupboard serves snacks;

Edwin No. 7 wears glasses from Edwin No. 2; pretending to be Mao in colors

Matisse No. 8 visits Ed Friedman No. 4;

Combined from Matador Cezanne; Carmen gores an aria;

Clobbers a postman with shoes of grass;

Translation of a cloud's tail; waits by cloud's night table;
Assisted by movements of art; from No. 4 all the way to Dada 4;
Peter Paul No.16 awaits in a bath of blood from World War 8;
Was that Word 8; World Wound perhaps; incomplete;
Scenarios; cousin plays for brother; if sing how come organ so plug;
Runs the gauntlet scared; Warlord No. 15 calls Avenue 5 Fifth;
Chanson Aznavour No. 2 revisits greatest triumph No. 3;
Greatest fall No. 7; greatest invention; greatest country of images;

> the greatest street in the world
> the greatest of all traffic lights
> is the one which catches the baseball cap
> of the boy running to catch the light
> the boy who catches light
> loses his life running to catch his cap
> the light who catches the boy
> is the greatest of all, changing
> in the middle of the street

I.E. ZAGMM

i.e.ZaGMM/1

˘ °GMM ¥á˘˘ °GMM¥á˘˘ °GMMPá˘˘ °GMMxá˘˘ °GMMZá˘˘ °MMM
˘ °GMMåá˘˘ °GMMZá˘˘ °GMM¥á˘˘ °GMMåá˘˘ °GMMZá˘˘ °MMM
˘ °GMMåá˘˘ °GMMåá˘˘ °GMMåá˘˘ °GMMåá˘˘ °GMMZá˘˘ °MMM
˘ °GMM'åá˘˘ °GMM åá˘˘ °GMMåá˘˘ °GMMåá˘˘ °GMM¥á˘˘ °MMM

˘ °GMMZá˘˘ °GMMá˘˘ °GMMá˘˘ °GMMPá˘˘ °GMM/åá˘˘ °MM
Pá˘˘ °GMMdá˘˘ °GMM(Zá˘˘ °GMMåá˘˘ °GMMåá˘˘ °GMMåá˘˘ °MM Zá˘
˘ °GMMåá˘˘ °GMMZá˘˘ °GMMåá˘˘ °GMMZá˘˘ °GMMZá˘˘ °MMM
Aåá˘˘ °GMMåá˘˘ °GMMåá˘˘ °GMMåá˘˘ °GMMdá˘˘ °GMMZá˘˘ °MMåá˘

˘ °GGG¥á˘˘ °GGG¥á˘˘ °GGG¥á˘˘ °GGGxá˘˘ °GGGxá˘˘ °MMM
˘xá˘˘ °GGGxá˘˘ °GGG!xá˘˘ °GGG?xá˘˘ °GGG.xá˘˘ °GGGxá˘˘ °MMM¥á˘
˘ °GGGZá˘˘ °GGG¥á˘˘ °GGGá˘˘ °GGG¥á˘˘ °GGGá˘˘ °GGG¥á˘˘ °MMM
˘Zá˘˘ °GGG¥á˘˘ °GGGZá˘˘ °GGGxá˘˘ °GGGxá˘˘ °GGG¥i˘˘ °MMMxá˘

xá˘˘ °¥á˘˘ °xá˘˘ °ná˘˘ °Zá˘˘ °x¥˘
x¥˘˘ °¥¥˘˘ °x¥˘˘ °n¥˘˘ °x¥˘˘ °o¥˘
¥¥˘ °¥¥˘˘˘ °x¥˘˘ °Mx¥˘˘ °Zx¥˘
¥¥˘x¥˘˘˘˘ o˘˘˘˘˘ o˘˘˘˘˘ o˘˘˘˘˘

˘ °MMMx¥˘˘ °MMMx¥˘˘°MMMå¥˘˘ °MMMåd˘˘ °MMMåd˘˘Ù °MMMåd˘
˘ °MMMån˘˘ °MMMZá˘˘ °MMMZá˘˘ °MMMån˘˘ °MMMZn˘˘ °MMMxn˘
˘ °MMM¥n˘˘ °MMMZn˘˘ °MMM¥n˘˘ °MMMZn˘˘ °MMM¥á˘˘ °MMM¥á

XÓ
kÓ˘˘
kÓ
XÓ

Ä

Through the blatant refusal
of insensitive truth,
                    and honesty's promise,
                              and reality's noose.
SEDUCER!?!
-si UNO! si DOS...es un "i.e. Seducer" Dolores?
...me-Dusas! -Si dueño...solares de rosas! -Dolares,
señoras? -One dollar, rose pesos!ò G6Bh\ èGdollar / juantala /
one dollar èG!Bh› çGù˘˘˘˘xx2»d˘˚–˘˘˘@pP˘˘y˘˘˘qstuvwx˘˘˘Å
˘˘˘åñ˘˘ °GMMå†˘˘ °GMMxx2ù˘˘˘˘xx2»d˘˚–˘˘˘˘   ?
        prrrrrrrrrrrrrrrrrrrrrrrrrrr
dos dios / two gods / two zeuses... < ZEUS, DUSA-ME∂Ô¯¿Íƒîƒíÿîì–˘˘
            ù˘˘˘˘xx2»
            d˘˚–˘˘˘˘˘
            ˘˘˘ °GMM
            MMe / a
            nd the NOH
            of outside
        O˘˘ñ the YOU / and the I / and that...
X˘˘˘˘˘˘@thexx2»d˘˚–˘˘˘˘?ù˘˘˘˘
¿@ @@Ä@@@¿@
            @@4Ä5¿@6¿¿7¿Ä8Ä@9Ä@>@@C@¿H¿@X@jÄÄl@l¿@
            m¿@v@Ç@ÄÉÄ@áÄ@àÄ@â@äÄ@å¿¿ëÄÄû@ÄüÄÄ
            †¿•¿¿´¿Ä∂ @@∂Ä∂ @¿øÄ@∂@Ä
            @@œÄ@'@¿Ú¿@˚@¿¿¿
Ä@@
¿
¿(Ä/@@>ÄH@]@¿ñ

@~@â/@¬ÄÄÁÄ¿ÏÄ

ÄVu1¿¶¿∂¿‰¿ ¿„›»MÎ(»M&ÄEÄ pesos!i˘˘˘˘∂ THEz@˘˘˘∂Ä˘˘ê

\ èG!Bê
›
/˘˘˘˘

i.e.ZaGMM/3

and the NOH of outside

yOT

±˘˘ö2»d˘°–˘˘/ TPFF˘˘ës will i.e. forever

oh my darling o©O   '

Ë

Ë˘˘âÙ¿˘˘ ! ¿˘˘ breathe believe and be B¥

(P

B¥·éP¥P¥–P¥†P¥pP¥

@ÓPB¥

(PB¥

(P∂Ä˘˘

P@
–`@`@–Æ-
P
–ÙP DuPê7
–@P@}¿
      @&"4P:P:â"–   "Î:Q–MSQP3L@@
      –Pê7
–>Å –;é– °o@3L@ êd@–@}@†2
PkZ@@
–@@
–IIIIIIIIIIIIIIIIIIIIIIIIIIIIIIIIIIIIIIIIIIIIIIIIIIIII!?9$êlzlz˘˘G˘˘HH˘˘˘˘r˘hn•˘˘ °GMMDés
Hollywood Du Jours

¿h
˘˘˘¸$êrr˘˘H¿ÄÄ@@   !Ä@Oh me, I should explore the realm of -
        Had it - gone!
        Oh - nope!
        There it - shit!
        My loofa -
oh!˘˘/X$AÎn•˘˘°GMMHH˘˘˘r¿Á+Ì∂ ' H˘˘MM˘˘˘0¸Î+?$ê6$6$˘˘N˘˘II˘˘˘
˘C !˘˘˘˘»ç¿!<$ê$$˘˘J˘
˘HH˘˘˘˘r¿œ!Ï'ì)|˘˘HH˘˘˘˘r¿
Ñ6:$êCC˘˘I˘˘HH˘˘˘˘rU@Îù˘˘˘˘xx2»d˘°–˘˘˘Ï'ì)|˘˘HH˘˘˘˘rOn•˘˘°GMMHH
˘˘˘˘r°GM!K./0123˘˘˘˘
Å†˘˘`á¿˘˘˘˘HH˘˘˘˘r‡7A$ō–˘˘P˘HH˘˘˘˘r® n•˘˘°GMMOO˘˘˘˘

i.e.AaZOO/5

® R"ÛX
® ÛX
® ShUVWXYZ``````ë`````m[\]^_``````Å````nabcdef````Å````oyz{|}~````Å`
```qstuvwx````Å````röÜáàâä````Å````vãåçéèê````Å````wëîúùû````Å`
```xü†°¢£§````Å````y•¶ß®©™````Å````z±∂∂¥µ∂````Å`````|¨∂ÆØ∂``
`Å`````}∂ ∂ π∂°````â````~012345````Å````Ä<=>?@A````Å````Ç$%&'()`
````Å````ÉBCEFST````Å````Ñ6789:;````Å````Ö∂ æø¿¡¬````Å````Ü…
ÀÃÕŒ````Å````àœ——
""'``````Å````â ÄÅÇÉÑ````Å````ä'÷∂ÿŸ/````Å````ã ⋄fifl‡````Å````åÁËÈÍÎ
Ï````â````é·,„‰ÂÊ````Å````êÌÓÔÒÚ````Å````ëÛÙı```````Å`````ï¨˙˝˛
``Å````î ````Å````ï````Å````ô∂ƒ∂∂«»````Å````õ
````

® ÛX® S:ICascaDéScrit3£Caslo3RomaCaslo540
Roma$enturyExpdBdItBT ExpdCenturyItBiT;ExpdBd
BT;ÆCentury;ItExpanded;ØlCent;UryOldSelfStyleItl:ZÃ˘˘ÄBFft
Bold: HelveticHeldCompressed9 BHelvetedLoveted
BolāBurialGeneci1SGothExtraFrankCond: 1+OFftOblique9ÛOFft
ObliqueBook:HellVenticObligeäFk∂Got;No.2 Goud∂ Time Cooch
I9;Ron_ch_BOFftBloodOblique: Fft9UHelvUltCompay9YGEN,evAMon;Garamo
Adamo8IA8AIt8IAGaramHissstero ExpiSemiblon:Itic8‰Aaramo
TiTling;flLAGaramineXpandexedBlooded 8ABololdHaremExposéd8ÊABaramo
ItI8AÄExpittedBlokHdItal8EAExpBId8EAGaraBlo8IA;ZaraBo;Itlit8IABaraGlond
Lital:Ic8,,ABragoABraMondSemiGlo;BloatA‰Baragold;Blade
SamaBlow8‡Aldine401BdIt BT ¿Aldine401It;I'll,BT SAldinee401Boo,booed
BT UAladine401 BT;áAnzeilglit#ÆNewArrgowSmallerCps
+NewArrwoMaidenRegularFrmCps#Undensed–New,RowBulow;Cond#TransBank#Go
HexMrdr RelatedBT ,BankGothic Lt Mrdr,BT +BernhMod a;œBirdlegsUsual;MrdSGŒBod,onli:MP
Body,nono-Poser:I,CascadeEnscrito3£Caslon3;Romanı 8Caslono54 Soso
O,Roman$Century,ExpdYrBldItal;BT Cent,uryExplodet CenturyBak;2Expd∂ Blood
BooTd;ÆCenturyExpitd BT;Øl CenturyExpound:Zra

@˘˘Ä

        ÛX

INTRINITE LINE

I, a triangle of, I
trinity for oasis
obscured by drought
I, a trinity of, so
geometric infinity
trapped by drink—
I choose to stand, not moving
to the infinite—so daring
in its line

is resistance if it is mine—

A NUYO-FUTURIST'S MANIFESTINY

•

EVER PUT
THE NEW IN YO?

FUTURISMO ISSA NOW ONLY HERE BUT IT IS ISN'T HERE YU KNO ?

:THE ALPHABET
EXPLONED/EXPLAINING
BETPHABETLA :
to **EXPLODE**
EXPLAIN the
transcape / the scope, of what
will be heard... to-noche / to-night!

ayyy...whattayawan'already?

my toong, **?** , m'haart, **?** , moo choong, **?** , *ka PUNK-PUNGA-PUNK* **!!!**

excuse me...I gotta answer the....

WHOODAT?
- *(voice from outside) OYE...'sta F-YOU-ture!*
YO ,WASSUP...MA-ÑA-NA-ME!
- *(voice from outside) OYE...mañana-NO, me llame fuTUra!*
YO, CHOOCHO GOLOOKY...PORQUE!?!

spanish is a fad   *to the puplik*
iif my *Panish* S a FAD to step on and present to the Uplik
untik-silver-biscocho-noche-cuaracha-coo...who's to say
mi PORTOCULTI PERPO don't sweat me a doopy
under mi unquestionable reliance on irrel-level-anting manipulations of lettras?   *bang*

que tu quiere: mi **GORDO?** mi **FAT?** mi **SIEGO?** mi **BILENGUA?**

I don't wanna creep into history a dismembered *essi-po-ican*, you know...
flipped by whippet johnnys and poopet judys while
isla's angelinos watch my cherubic-é-steps'PORTing my TRIBE-oricuan-STRIIIIDE

AFRICANO MAN...MO-FA-SI-BRO / I MEAN AMMA'RICAN...I KNO YU NO / I MEAN I'M AN ISLAND...YA SLO YA BLO HEXICANO-CHICO-CUBANO-RICO / CABEZA QUE NO CONOCZA'I YO LLEGO / GO GALLO DE RISO MAYO SOY SAPO DE POTPURRI... / GORDO-FAT-SIEGO-BLIND / BORICUA-IS-PUERTORICAN-FOR-PUERTORICO

AYYYY: soy gordo...pero GORDISSIMO!...de nada.

> : QUESTIONS
> OF / **AURAL** EXTENSION : 'xploding will 'xplain
> but *explaining* will *explone*
> in volume...the FACT, of a question!   *experienco presentado en dos ways*
>
> ───────────────────
>
> That I ask / for the SAKE of asking : **BECOMES**
> an *extension* of language : **APPEARING** : as writing!
> : ALPHABET EXPLODES ITSELF :
> the Stem issa stroke   down from the inside
>   to fall out of
>   and when inside...
> impossible to explain!   **WHEN** : does invention
> become language?

What difference between outside forces forcing the trip and inside forces
creating the trip the ground catches us the brusie is what we remember
How many *trips* before a safe journey...no safe journeys   *revolu descarga y tombé pompu*

> **DOG** is **DOG** : as I see it
> someone will notice his legs : I will notice his head
>   what is the possibility of being an elephant : as dog
>   or being a fountainhead   because I know of   R. MUTT

The seed being grown - the world inside
This growing has no obstacle no question whether the world inside
will ever equal the one outside, it won't...it will always be much much bigger

AYYYY: soy flaco...pero FLACISSIMO!...de nada.
mira me...

toktoktok-talk talkin' that tickly talk

───────────────────

FAT-BUT-FATTISSIMO! / SKINNY-BUT-SKINNISSIMO! / OF-NOTHING / WHAT-EXPLODES-FROM-ITSELF / DO-I
EXPLODE-AS-I-BORN-MYSELF / IF-I-SPIT-ON-MY-PISS-IS-THE-CONNECTION-VITAL / IF-BOTH-ARE-THROWN
IN-THE-WIND-WHICH-WILL-COME-BACK-FASTER / IS-SPEED-THE-POINT / OR-IS-IT-THICKNESS / WEIGHT

sacred naked ün jiggly vault

my figgly fills out my vision of me

as a Cosmo Girl! *elevanté*

- *(voice from outside)* **OYE, trend-o-bulous and fab-o-mundo,!,**

Fitt-a-in though,?,

NAAA-Don't WANNO,!,

Wanna NOMbra-me HOMbra-me HEH...HEH...HOY!

oooohhh that's soooooooooo...HERE!

: AND MAYBE THAT says something about my

here : SAYING SOMETHING ABOUT *yours*

: COMPARED TO YOUR *is*

uncertain it is...*who is it, you're talking to,?,*

---

your very 'uture F - *which implies change -*

which is not security - which is never past -

which is not change - which has just passed

which is only - here *whew!*

Y ahora, esta bueno?   Si, si...esta bueno.

BLIP! blippin!

That radar creepin' for the *new* thing!

O there I am...in solitary *OYE-ME*

singing Accapaella Oceanary 'emory 'ainbows

O there I am...dismembered in *what-I-see's*

smelling the "new thing" in the air

GOBS-OF-LIQUID-WEIGHT-IN-TIME / TRAVELING-TO-MY-FACE-VISITING-THE-PLACE-IT-CAME-FROM / COME-BACK
SPIT-PISS-COME-BACK-TO-IT / MY-PAST-SINCE-IT'S-MY-MEMORY / MY-TOMORROW-SINCE-I-WAS-YOUNGER
AND-NOW-IS-GOOD? / YES-NOW-IS-GOOD / SUMMARY-IS-NOT-NEW / AHHH-TO-BE-SAINTISSIMO-OF-NOTHING!

- **No new thing in this PANG-slish.**
- **No samo-samo in these creeks.**
- **This *these's* notta *say***
  catching pieces of *broken* says, *spoken* species.

NU-YO-essi-PO-you-can YOU SAY...
  decipherous glowing wormy glypherous?
howyousay-ro-lyphics - *chuga zucre* -
  como se dice - OLE! -

AYYYY:

the footnote to pure experience...the beginning of new experience

whattaya wan'...already?

.aural extension of tongue is page.	.from the inside. an explosion.
.to lick for licking. to ask for asking.	.and once inside.
.stroke your letter.	.impossible to explain.

oye Calcachipando con Pernir...que tu quiere?

mi visiones con barbed wire veins?
bleeding little seeds, little treasures?
  little shatters of *what-you-thinks*?

Soy siego...pero SIEGISSIMO!...de nada.

...mira me...
...looking for a...PATRIO-TOE-TAP kinda swing...

check it out

...once uponna visit downtown...
...tar-beach-baby-brown-cousins, looking at this...
...uptown-maybe-brown-ain't-one-of-us...A-very-cano-'Mericano...
...brand-new-baby-new no fad...kids that age, you know...in constant constant...
...maybe no-name-shy shoots a "who-you-lookin'-at" glance at this...
...uptown-maybe-brown-cousin...baby-brown-eyes lock in...
...checking each out, shooting daggers, living-room island corners, their corners to mine...

I-ARRIVE-HERE-TOMORROW-AND-I-LEAVE-YESTERDAY / FOR-TODAY-I'M-FOREVER-AND-IT'S-HERE-THAT-I'LL-STAY
I-CAN-SEE-WHERE-I'M-STANDING-WHERE-MY-SHADOW-BEGINS / THERE'S-A-PULL-TO-THE-OCEAN-WHERE-MY
SHADOW-HAS-BEEN / IN-THE-STRUCTURE-OF-RESTRUCTURING-WHERE-DO-JOURNEYS-OF-CONTROLLED-TRIPPING

HOMBRE!!! NOMBRA ME!!!   ...POW-POW...

Ohhhh...tu hurt your *tu*?

        Ohhhh...you wanna walk

            all over my mispronounciation of histrounounciacion -

               halcion chegger too?   *ayyy niño*

-*(voice from inside)* **" Don't yu know**

        rubbing away too many dreams

        only gives yu some *sing* iin yur *I* ?"

                  esta soñando? listen Pultropita...

       If you rub away : much-many-sleeps

       Deep away : claps-many-claps...you'll see

       Music-of-day lilo-siloquies   *tick-second-tock-tick*

          (approach your zzz's, baby-brown-zzz's)

               ...you'll see

       Many-much-middles gather 'round the age of recollection

listen Salchicha...

Something NOW is THIS : but there is no TIME
All the time : SOMETHING happens   over there...

        ...see!

      Rage REVOLUTES rage!

      Mañana is a MAN, viscous through withered pulse

      I am POROUS in my mañana-gown! Listen

      whatever time is in you, *too many got away!*

      If you RUB AWAY Boog, Bog and Blame...

      many-much-middles will shuck destiny within their finger-things

      and RUN AWAY!

      Somewhere anywhere DAYS by the truckload will RIP

      in typhonic-membrane-thunder-slap gallop!

      OCEANS opaque 'n take the shape of your eye!

SCATTER / PSSST-ONNA-STRETCH-THROUGH-WHATEVER-TIME-IS-IN-YOU-I-SAW-YOU-TURN-THE-PAGE...

Some MIDDLE is lost...encircled in upside-down-acceptance
ENCOURAGED by the hooves of sandmen who arrive a day late!
Oh...who rubbed away too many moons, huh?
Tarry soft upon the SUN-PUNK for one year
the Same-Thing-Time says the same thing!

the same thing sez the same thing

WE ARE IN "SAME-THING-TIME"...ALL THE TIME!!!
And something IS in your I...

o hosanna man ojo water man

see	the	rain
then	hear	it
hear	the	rain
then	feel	it
feel	the	rain
then	smell	it
smell	the	rain
then	taste	it
close	your	eyes
and	taste	the
a	i	r
the		rain
will		follow

you set up
different precedents
as a part of
your senses
the other senses
will follow

establish possibility
to allow
exploration
to allow
unexpectation
to happen

POSSIBILITY COMES FROM (TO)
PRECEDENCE BIRTHS
CONFIDENCE GIVES TO (OF)
POSSIBILITY GOES (AND)
TO (FROM) PRECEDENCE
BIRTHS CONFIDENCE (BORN) GIVES
(TO) (REPEAT)

i'm
strong enough
to blow you
away

i'm
strong enough
to breathe you
in

95

You paint pictures across the angles in light swarms.
It seems like some long Sundays ago.

Red Glazed Toreador. Spanking Sundays in the foyer.
Eye Level. Table Top Timiny. Everyday Across.

Geometric. Plane One to Planal Shift.
Oro Lindo. Lovely Saint Sunset.

Dark Hours Shower Us.
Night Screams Me In.

Anonimé...quiere caminar mi, none tierra firme?

Memory is : involuntary
Pre-verbal in : the everyday

I used to DO this   I used to BE this   I TELL you   I KNOW this!   or I used to

it was two dreams. kinda like a dream-ful vision from this morning. was broken. I think. like coming to from a deep that you're in. you know. kinda like half there. out of it but not really. one half to each other so where your never was. was where you were where I seams to live. pacifiers. a day-late quilt. tornados. in the corner of my eye.

River sly. Mouth Gender-talia.
Yo, s'uppilly slight lips...by the chance of sing.

Cun-cun-sexual-runt.
Nothlee-not-in-spit-ting.

Squar-cles in shadow dreams.
Outside...the animals make noise.

My earth is the one that revolves
                    inside my feet, where my toes
search for gravity, while my heel
                    trounces the heavens

OYE-MEEEEEEEE   (YEH)

I am pulled into it
screaming against what pulls me into it
I grab   I have fits   against sleep   shatters shape
I grab   against what   in spaces and crevices   I am not

until these words   find their space   and claim it
forever theirs   *see feel taste them*

this word and *this* word are no *these* words
they are *this* word and *this* word
and will always share
the moment they came together
as *soulmates* for a moment
in lifetime's forever

WORDS : *as* : **SOULMATES** : are the strongest deity
and a belief in them   will settle
the universes   inside you   *you...you...you-ingly as only you can*

OYE-IIEEOOUUUU   (YEH)

as LANGUAGE is : what creates us
let's create something greater : than
                    you or I
                    let's create us

MAÑANA-IS-TOMORROW / AYER-IS-YESTERDAY / HOY-IS-TODAY / BOG-IS-BLAME-IS-BOOG-IS / SEE-THEN-HEAR-
THEN-FEEL-THEN-SMELL-THEN-THE-HEAR-THE-FEEL-THE-SMELL-THE-TASTE-RAIN-IT-RAIN-IT-RAIN-IT-RAIN-IT /
PREGUNTA-IS-QUESTION / OYE-IS-LISTEN / DOUBLE-L-IS-YA-YA / PLAYA-IS-BEACH / NEW-IS-OTHER / WHAT-IS

Between night and twi'
I had only many look aways
I had one that did not look away
disappearing deep from where the music comes from
tall in the after in the small of *say*

*in the core of CORA-ROW-SI pipo, my
cora-boricua-nazion, zi
che che no leche, flows boucharon LOW below me*   *...there I am*

My questions stitch *says* I saw
in the day of *today* had
a curtain pulled from T.O.D.A.
left me Y they...
    certainly queria llamarme "mañana" ayer...aqui...
no hay nada...mas que briza...

*the day comes down ripped of tongue
este DIA descends me torn de lengua
toronado...tengo nada...ayyy...que briza
toronado...tengo nada...ayyy...que briza*

when is best time to tell someone when something is ending. at what point do you
become ready to accept change. this ending is a break with what's happening. at the
moment it happens. the point of change to begin something new. the point of change
to end something old. the space created between the two. is where begin comes from.
vibrations of change permeate the air. stillness becomes sound. voice. pen. paper. old
stillness maybe years old. becomes an image of how something existed. in that space.
a charged stillness which space has yet to let go of. sometimes difficult to accept change
in that space. so time takes over. time is the assistant to space. time helps space when
neccesary to change an old memory. string breaks together. forms a greater space
to place time in. no best time for anything. many breaks in time. many endings.
this is just one of them.

CROSSING / THEY-CALL-TOMORROW-YESTERDAY-HERE / TORNADO-I-HAVE-NOTHING / BUT-WHATTA-BREEZE /
NOW-I-FALL-WHERE-IT'S-EMPTY-WHERE-THE-DAY-WANTS-TO-BE / WHERE-I-LOSE-MY-TOMORROW-AND-IT'S-HERE
THAT-I'M-FREE / THERE'S-A-RIBBON-IN-SUNLIGHT-A-RIP-IN-THE-SKY / AND-IT-STRANGLES-FOREVER

THE DESIGN OF LANGUAGE : the senses	
A	A LANGUAGE OF MOVEMENT
E	A LANGUAGE OF SOUND
I	A LANGUAGE OF VISION
O	A LANGUAGE OF TASTE
U	A LANGUAGE OF TOUCH
Y	A LANGUAGE OF SMELL
Z	A LANGUAGE OF MEANING

structures of possible
restructuring

journeys of controlled
'tripping'

journeys of uncontrolled
'tripping'

seeds scattered
according to obstacles

children are the precedent for creation
animals are the precedent for migration
erosion the precedent for emotion
the spoken present awoken

If I am to tailor the rips of heaven let me do so at my own_____.
But there's kinda this Blue Heavy over everything and even though's and
others that cast a fall on hope lack of hope
and even though ever is in everything
you would not want to control it all...you could not control it.
Would it stay asleep if I keep it in
if I don't sleep if it stays in me...sleeps for me so
I don't sleep.
I don't sleep.
I'll sleep. I don't sleep.
Would it be possible to lie if I say it I'm lying
and ever would be everything.
If I don't know...then
which eye is
sleepless endless...then
is my I.

ONE-DAY-AT-A-TIME

the sun cannot be reproduced, only represented - cezanne
the sun can be entered, only in poetry - torres/mayakovsky

word contorts - hobo words
early words - child words
brutal alchemist of perfect words - words as culture brought together in one word
the animal who cannot speak like a man - as a shadow of his silence

you create this space which has no content. a place where morning is life and death is day. an architecture of ritual as cyclical as breath. through revisiting the healing progresses. is healing needed. yes. why. because life is painful. it reminds us of our time left. this is fine because we are healed. because we find our space. and claim it. forever ours.

Pero...I say I see through the velvet campasia de mi...

1. **And I see that I say I am soy muy flaco de HOY...**

2. **That I tear through palabras con mi muy Fuerza de Rico...**

3.. **That I rip apart THAT that prevents me from speak...**

4. **That I TEAR through mañanas...through ME sometimes...ME!!!**

O poor *me*
for fear of being PO-nouned
esie-poesie-nouned   futur   uture   suture
I have placed myself into the middles   *no place to be*
into the street that I am
by the force of evening, I am breathing one large room
somewhere in your i   *look at my lettras*

PERO-BUT / CAMPASIA-COUNTRYSIDE / PALABRAS-YU-KNO / WHO-GETS-THIS-IF-THERE-ISN'T-A-WHO-THERE / SO-COME-TO-ME-DARLING-AND-RESCUE-ME / I'VE-LIVED-HERE-FOREVER-BUT-I-CAN'T-BREATHE / TOMORROW MIGHT-SAVE-ME-BUT-I-CAN'T-SEE / SO-COME-TO-ME-DARLING-AND-RESCUE-ME

meridean gets thrown against the plates
sunspot skull gets splayed out - equator to tummy

like a riding
hiding nomad
always
in gallows' insatiate hunger
galloping...
galloping...
siempre golpando el mundo...
that is...*always*
hurting the
when the too simple to stitch-titch-the
when the
DIA he calls me to fix-RIP the
when the
DAY calls me to fix-RIP the
when the
DAY I RIP IT - THE
DAY I RIP - APART
la DIA she calls me to
FIX. RIP.
A. FIX.   RIP. IT.
THE   DAY
RIPPIT -   THE - DAY .
RIPPIT -   THE - DAYDAY .
RIPPIT - I RIP. A FIX.
            as IF. I COULD FIX. A RIP - A DAY
  I DAY -
with a stitch - with

            ...ayyyy canito...salio lindo...
...LalaLALA la LAla LA--LalaLALA la LAla LA...

SOLITARY-FIGUREHEAD / ROAMING-THE-WOUND / SEARCHING-AT-ONCE-DESTROYING / INNA-FIELD-OF-DAYS
SIEMPRE-IS-ALWAYS / WHAT-COMES-FROM-ANOTHER-MOUTH / MODIFIES-THE-SAYING-OF-IT / IN-YOURS /
LITTLE-ONE / YOU-CAME-OUT-PRETTY / SHE-SINGS-HER-SONG / MERIDEAN-IS-MERCATOR'S-PROJECTION

Se FUE! EL DIA! : : : : : :WEPA!!!!

QUE PASO?   WUPPENCE?

your sun ripped...your moon a scar...let me see...QUICK

kick the day...back to tickle...the roof the tongue goes:

!UT! : !WUT! : !FUUSENTLY YUP! : !RUT! :

UNO : : : clump poal : ! OLÉ ! : clampout - puut 't'it out - too :

DOS : : : BULL de mi towers SING ringa ding-DINGS :

TRES : : : torres SIN toro OLÉ!

AYYYY : : : I never grew up how you might imagine

Put down *the man* get over. Be the man *get real*. Do it til you get it *AGAIN*.
Put down *the man* get over. Be the man *get real*. Do it til you get it *AGAIN*.

Oh portray poor child! Poor stereotype!
Oh barrio de los blancos! Cockroach corner princess!
Oh domino playing machismo! Allover himself!
Oh mami's face! Isla de mi vida!
Oh force me to SIN - verguenza all over my
S. P : : : anish
QUI : : : uerto
REE : : : eople

Soy gringo...pero GRINGISSIMO...de nada!

---

what becomes imagined from outward to inward thought. becomes reconfigured to represent new free thought. to the myth the idle of mythter in new light. quoting a world's freedom. here are some words in a time of finality. here is my final association with searching.

YORICUA-IS-OLD / AS-OLD-AS-RICO / WHO-DESIRES-NEW-INVENTS-NU / EX-PATRIOT-CONFUSIO-REALIGNS
WITH-SUN / FOOTNOTE-FOR-DESPAIR-BECOMES-SHADOW / AHHH-TO-BE-SHADDISSIMO-OF-NOTHING!

We are haloed becuz
we find our sun we shine
O lovely lettras giving it all
Here in my pen
there is the sky...O haloed buzz
find my sun, tell me I will shine
in my letters again   *yup-yup-bo-ticklo-tock-tock*

---

in a land of sound the consonant is king
                    ...(TIMBRE)...
in a language of sound the mainstream is quiet
                    ...(TIMBRE-TIMBRE)...
in a landing of sound the ground is falling
                    ...('ELLO!)...
in a lending of sound the vowel is jester
                    ...('LO!)...

Earth Lamps d'eligio get planted one by
planets' watch, one by
the HIGH one
Galaxies clap in distant sobs, one by
slow one

Rhythm Po-Ri glistens
Sula-Mio sacred tincture
Tor-kon-Turra Sorro-Fillio turns against the open evening
Sands ascend me, saline 'capella

Time comes, gets me much over
Time trains that *samo-samo* EAR bell...into

WHOP! BOT! kinna-may-may-goose-bump : HUP! HUP!

and the hour makes you wonder

R'ELIGIO-VISITS-NEVER-HAVING-LEFT / GAP-WARRIOR-GETS-BRAIN-PUNCHED / PLANETS-ALIGN-INNA-FIELD
OF-LORDS / OCEAN-REMINDS-BEACH-OF-SHORE / EROSION-INVITES-MEMORY / CLAVÉ-VISITS-SÓN-SOL-SOLA /

If you're witnessing the disintegration of a friend?
Or is what disintegrates only change?

> Are YOU disintegrating?
> Into saviorhood?
> Totalto-lomente?

> *Si no tiene problema?*
> How you gonna treat Choo-Choo-Go-Lightly
> iif m' brother only sheds light on the up
> Haus...Arte gonna be a...Nada?

AYYYY: soy bilingual...pero BILINGUALISSIMO!...de nada!

diga me

> possiblo / resultos
> possivos / resuulloos
> posso / therefo / pooso
> resoloto / thereemino / rosoluuuluu

como se dice

: **JARGON** / of / **BRUSH** :
technically profficient irony exults thada spiritus / youth said *once*
how many years ago / was in the air of zoos / the godless names /
sort of planned / sort of helped / holy movement / essential cabaret /
considered criticisim / completely uninformed february / large glass /
hindenberg opportunist / before the war was a glass / large glass /
wedding of glass / ideas of ass / time / timo / timitio / mimimo /

> my mess is an unkept memory
> invented for unkept memorias, unslept palabrias, y para la hora mia
> everytime the world...

PUNKS-PUNGA-PUNK! on my door:

THE-H-IS-SILENT / THE-PEOPLE-AREN'T / PERDONNA-ME-I-DIDN'T-MEAN-TO-GO-THERE / TAKE-THIS-ALL-OF-YOU
ONE-OUNCE-OF-SAVIORHOOD-BUCKLED-BY-SANTERIA / ONE-FUNK-OF-PF-FLYERS-BATTERED-BY-TONTERIA / ONE
BOOTED-BOOTY-BOOSTED-BY-A-BEELZEBOB / BLINDED-BY-TIMEPIECE-RADIATE / WAVIORHOOD-CRAVES-SAKI-POUNCE

-WHOODAT?

-AYYYY, it's me!

-ZZZZO!-OUNZ!-EROS ON SPOLLO...'tsa small stoopid man
and a GIANT POLLO CON DONGO!   *MATA LA QUICK!!!*

-AYYYY, I wanna ya want already!

-Well, ya can't have it. I'm still
reconnaiss-sayin' a JA-vayzee DE joujou WOOK!
LOOK! BooBooMoMutton butts a chicken freak-head,
lapping dismal solvents into cranial jam!

-AYYYY, but it's me...IT's ME!!!

-HEYYYY, my here is now, joo-jo cookie.
GO la loop and STOOP yer chingo!

Essi-polican no wanna be big row GO up to: dult-a-pup. **(rufff)**

Po-ri presents ONE possibility: **(pant-pant-pant)**

What kind of WANT allows one to WANT to

salivante and ramble on, the incessant mongerer...eh? **(grrrrrrrrr)**

Como che diche, this "praise for ears"...eh? **(whine-whine)**

esta NOMAAAADO...eh? Diciendo AAAAALGO...eh?

guarango anglo

Guaguanco Anglo-ANNNNNNNNN-gloooo

pssst...ever put the new in yo?

Po-ri wants only a listen...a sp(l)ace to ME in, you know?
NUYO? YOU...YO...YEH   I don't,.   Know,.
No don't...why,. I question,.   why might,.   take the curve

out

of question

put the...

OYE-MEEEEEEE back in...SECURE in its bang!

WHEW! / ONLY-A-LISTEN-INDEED / EXCLAMATORY-IS-BANG / GUAGUANCO-IS SHAKING-YOUR-HIPS-IN-SALSA-TIME / DICIENDO-IS-TALKING / ANGLO-IS-ANGLES / A-POLLO-CLUCKS / A-PERO-BARKS / A-PORI-LISTENS / AND-WAY-UP-ABOVE / A-SLY-NOD-TO-ARMSTRONG-AND-FLAN / TAINO-MAN-LIVES-IN-YORICUA / NEO-RICO-IS-HERE

105

I fear : : : when I become secure in my bang : : : my what will stop
you see : : : DE NADA : : :
my nothing *which is applicable in two languages*
will either no! or !no

---

this quantum of poets on cellphone
this quatrain bailed out by wording hoods
slamming sungods onna brighter day
let me mouth out your sun-daupled cheeks dancing the eye's brow
sprinkle 5th grade devils onna sojourn from conspiracy
a pop star popping - celestial ink....no mere visible chart
but an open vowel for the minded
only this - as loud as motor lets - will be cosmology...
a refrain as old as me

But I say it is isn't the day
back a day ago where my day sits *el canyon es dulce*

Si, soy flaco...pero FLACCISSIMO!...de hoy...
looka me,

Rompa me
tira me
abráza me...AYER!

Chupa me
alma me
embrúta me...MAÑANA!

Sometimes I am the first to admit I need
the gilded claws of corn whippets *el otro es nuevo*
stitching *todays*
one by one.

I-BELIEVE-IN-TOMORROW-BUT-SHE-CAN'T-SEE-ME / I-WOULD-TELL-HER-THAT-I-LOVE-HER-BUT-SHE-CAN'T-HEAR
ME / THERE-IS-BEAUTY-IN-MOTION-IN-THE-AIR-THAT-I-NEED / BUT-I-CAN'T-FIND-THE-OCEAN-OR-THE-STARS
OR-THE-TREES / SO-COME-TO-ME-DARLING-AND-RESCUE-ME / I'VE-LIVED-HERE-FOREVER-BUT-I-CAN'T-BREATHE

Other times...

I say I *soy* the last to see that

to see others' *say* that

haven't been *placed*

in *me* places

heaven hasn't had *sees* for new says

me *new* say-places...

elevate the ask.

my pregunta pauses into essi-porico decipherous unintelligible to belligible pillows...

Yoose Haus? Arte Nada?
Alivertann Ginseltinne's torquee...howls POON tow ! OLÉ!
Udder-Franco, chenchi's mi Hara-cora Row-marilla!
Sun's UBER shower's baila la brilla...'dilo'dilock junkets!
Hierolypliks-HerramanOPkiks-TockloTockTicks.

Fincas de memorias

touchdown alightly vibrates

A hammock torn. A day-lindo. Lying on broken palabras.

Una playa. Un niño.

...salio lindo, canito..."

I-DIA

My-DAY

Now-HERE

The idea of-NOW YOU GOT IT...

This t'oong.

This h'aart...M 'choong...

kaPUNK-kaPUNGA-kaPUNK

oYE-ME

yOU-me

YO-yeh...

TOMORROW-MIGHT-SAVE-ME-BUT-I-CAN'T-SEE / TOMORROW-IS-DROWNING-IN-WHAT-I-SEE / TOMORROW
I-PROMISE-I'LL-LET-YOU-SEE

YEAH, YOU KNOW...YOU
Neo-Nuyo...this is...NEO-RICO!

The "new" - as a *pastele* (a place, newly-rich...*sort of...*)
The "sort of" - as a concept (nebulous to outsiders, indifferent to, the *other...*)
The "other" - as Neo-Rico...you know...a Nuyo-stupor (a staple diet of manifestos...)

Many - Festinies, stirred by my Fists of Destiny!
My - Fast - Tiny - Fists!
My - Night - Festivities!
My - Nice - NUYO - Cities!
A dent of the - I - of me
                    MY - dentity - fies
The "here"   ...*WEPA!*
                    and it's a different HERE

        Not the HERE you know   it's a different THERE
Not the THERE you DON'T know...you
        aren't ever THERE   you say WHAT you say to IT
                                    IT no longer is

ONCE you know   answer LIVES to
        WHAT you know   ANSWER lives to
WANT   for OTHER answer   LIES to form
        ONE other answer   LOST to Wonder - forever...   *(awwwwww)*

        You LOST you You knows you You say who Who calls you
        You knows YOU (who knew you) You lost WHO Lost who I
        Lost I CALL you You say WHO knew you knew KNOW "new" NO
        No NEW knew You no YOU no NUYO Neo-Say you who CALL
        Say you I YOU NO YOU Rico New LOST you Call you...   lost me!

Once I CALL you "new"   I KNOW you
        Once I KNOW you   you LOST you
What you call NEW   call I ONCE
        I CALL you   I used to NU-YO you...who? YOYU!

SAY who lost who Who calls who I? Says WHO - I say
You? Says ME - I know WHO I know *Whoah*...says I yo
NEO-why KNOW who say NO you say ME I see WHY
Know NUYO know YOU...   NUYO know ME?

YO - YEH - *ME*   YO - YEH - *ME*
        YOYO - *YEH*   ME - ME - *FAH*
                YEH - YEH - *LO - CO - SOY*   YOYO - *FAR*
                        YEH - I - *GO*   F - F - *FAR*
                                YEH - I - *GO*   F - F - *FAR*
I - I - I   S - S - SAY   M - M - MY   S - S - SEA
        I - I - IS   A - A - A   L - L - LIGHT
                M - M - MY   L - L - LIGH'   T - T - T
I - I - IS   TH - TH - THE   T - T - TIME
                M - M - MY   L - L - LI'   T - T - T
I - I - IS   TH - TH - THE   T - T - TIME
        TH - TH - THE   T - T - T
                TH - TH - TH   T - T - T...
                        TH - TH - TH...   T - T - T...
                                T - T - T...   T - T - T...

finaltolores

109

ROOF BOOKS

Andrews, Bruce. **Co**. Collaborations with Barbara Cole, Jesse Freeman, Jessica Grim, Yedda Morrison, Kim Rosefield. 104p. $12.95.

Andrews, Bruce. **Ex Why Zee**. 112p. $10.95.

Andrews, Bruce. **Getting Ready To Have Been Frightened**. 116p. $7.50.

Benson, Steve. **Blue Book**. Copub. with The Figures. 250p. $12.50

Bernstein, Charles. **Controlling Interests**. 80p. $11.95.

Bernstein, Charles. **Islets/Irritations**. 112p. $9.95.

Bernstein, Charles (editor). **The Politics of Poetic Form**. 246p. $12.95; cloth $21.95.

Brossard, Nicole. **Picture Theory**. 188p. $11.95.

Cadiot, Olivier. **Former, Future, Fugitive**. Translated by Cole Swensen. 166p. $13.95.

Champion, Miles. **Three Bell Zero**. 72p. $10.95.

Child, Abigail. **Scatter Matrix**. 79p. $9.95.

Davies, Alan. **Active 24 Hours**. 100p. $5.

Davies, Alan. **Signage**. 184p. $11.

Davies, Alan. **Rave**. 64p. $7.95.

Day, Jean. **A Young Recruit**. 58p. $6.

Di Palma, Ray. **Motion of the Cypher**. 112p. $10.95.

Di Palma, Ray. **Raik**. 100p. $9.95.

Doris, Stacy. **Kildare**. 104p. $9.95.

Doris, Stacy. **Cheerleader's Guide to the World: Council Book** 88p. $12.95.

Dreyer, Lynne. **The White Museum**. 80p. $6.

Dworkin, Craig. **Strand**. 112p. $12.95.

Edwards, Ken. **Good Science**. 80p. $9.95.

Eigner, Larry. **Areas Lights Heights**. 182p. $12, $22 (cloth).

Gardner, Drew. **Petroleum Hat**. 96p. $12.95.

Gizzi, Michael. **Continental Harmonies**. 96p. $8.95.

Gladman, Renee. **A Picture-Feeling**. 72p. $10.95.

Goldman, Judith. **Vocoder**. 96p. $11.95.

Gottlieb, Michael. **Ninety-Six Tears**. 88p. $5.

Gottlieb, Michael. **Gorgeous Plunge**. 96p. $11.95.

Gottlieb, Michael. **Lost & Found**. 80p. $11.95.

Greenwald, Ted. **Jumping the Line**. 120p. $12.95.

Grenier, Robert. **A Day at the Beach**. 80p. $6.

Grosman, Ernesto. **The XULReader: An Anthology of Argentine Poetry (1981–1996)**. 167p. $14.95.

Guest, Barbara. **Dürer in the Window, Reflexions on Art**. Book design by Richard Tuttle. Four color throughout. 80p. $24.95.

Hills, Henry. **Making Money**. 72p. $7.50. VHS videotape $24.95. Book & tape $29.95.

Huang Yunte. **SHI: A Radical Reading of Chinese Poetry**. 76p. $9.95

Hunt, Erica. **Local History**. 80 p. $9.95.

Kuszai, Joel (editor) **poetics@**, 192 p. $13.95.

Inman, P. **Criss Cross**. 64 p. $7.95.

Inman, P. **Red Shift**. 64p. $6.

Lazer, Hank. **Doublespace**. 192 p. $12.

Levy, Andrew. **Paper Head Last Lyrics**. 112 p. $11.95.

Mac Low, Jackson. **Representative Works: 1938–1985**. 360p. $18.95 (cloth).

Mac Low, Jackson. **Twenties**. 112p. $8.95.
McMorris, Mark. **The Café at Light**. 112p. $12.95.
Moriarty, Laura. **Rondeaux**. 107p. $8.
Neilson, Melanie. **Civil Noir**. 96p. $8.95.
Osman, Jena. **An Essay in Asterisks**. 112p. $12.95.
Pearson, Ted. **Planetary Gear**. 72p. $8.95.
Perelman, Bob. **Virtual Reality**. 80p. $9.95.
Perelman, Bob. **The Future of Memory**. 120p. $14.95.
Piombino, Nick, **The Boundary of Blur**. 128p. $13.95.
Prize Budget for Boys, **The Spectacular Vernacular Revue**. 96p. $14.95.
Raworth, Tom. **Clean & Will-Lit**. 106p. $10.95.
Robinson, Kit. **Balance Sheet**. 112p. $11.95.
Robinson, Kit. **Democracy Boulevard**. 104p. $9.95.
Robinson, Kit. **Ice Cubes**. 96p. $6.
Rosenfield, Kim. **Good Morning—MIDNIGHT—**. 112p. $10.95.
Scalapino, Leslie. **Objects in the Terrifying Tense Longing from Taking Place**. 88p. $9.95.
Seaton, Peter. **The Son Master**. 64p. $5.
Shaw, Lytle. The Lobe. 80 p. $11.95
Sherry, James. **Popular Fiction**. 84p. $6.
Silliman, Ron. **The New Sentence**. 200p. $10.
Silliman, Ron. **N/O**. 112p. $10.95.
Smith, Rod. **Music or Honesty**. 96p. $12.95
Smith, Rod. **Protective Immediacy**. 96p. $9.95
Stefans, Brian Kim. **Free Space Comix**. 96p. $9.95
Tarkos, Christophe. **Ma Langue est Poétique—Selected Works**. 96p. $12.95.
Templeton, Fiona. **Cells of Release**. 128p. with photographs. $13.95.
Templeton, Fiona. **YOU—The City**. 150p. $11.95.
Torres, Edwin. **The All-Union Day of the Shock Worker**. 112 p. $10.95.
Tysh, Chris. **Cleavage**. 96p. $11.95.
Ward, Diane. **Human Ceiling**. 80p. $8.95.
Ward, Diane. **Relation**. 64p. $7.50.
Watson, Craig. **Free Will**. 80p. $9.95.
Watten, Barrett. **Progress**. 122p. $7.50.
Weiner, Hannah. **We Speak Silent**. 76 p. $9.95
Weiner, Hannah. **Page**. 136 p. $12.95
Wellman, Mac. **Miniature**. 112 p. $12.95
Wellman, Mac. **Strange Elegies**. 96 p. $12.95
Wolsak, Lissa. **Pen Chants**. 80p. $9.95.
Yasusada, Araki. **Doubled Flowering: From the Notebooks of Araki Yasusada**. 272p. $14.95.

ROOF BOOKS are published by
Segue Foundation • 300 Bowery •New York, NY 10012
Visit our website at **segue.org**

ROOF BOOKS are distributed by
SMALL PRESS DISTRIBUTION
1341 Seventh Avenue • Berkeley, CA. 94710-1403.
Phone orders: 800-869-7553
spdbooks.org